The Storm Inside

Orange County is in Southeast Texas on Sabine Lake at the Gulf of Mexico.

The Storm Inside: Poetry & Prose by High School Students in Orange County, Texas

LITERARY PRESS
LAMAR UNIVERSITY

Table of Contents

Poetry

Fictional Prose

Personal Narratives

Academic Essays

Preface by Kate Williams

This volume is a rare opportunity to listen to high school students talking about two interrelated problems: extreme weather and inequality. One of the very real effects they name is *The Storm Inside*. Nationwide, surveys and professionals report that mental health support is young people's number one request, at college level and younger. *The Storm Inside* is a terribly widespread phenomenon. This is so whether your town experiences floods or fires, heat waves or deep freezes, hurricanes or tornadoes.

Thomas Szasz argued that the task of mental health professionals is to help people talk through what he called "problems of daily living," of their own free will, with mutual respect, with as much confidentiality as needed, and so on. These young people are practicing this here with their poetry and prose. *The Storm Inside* insists that we listen, or we'll all go nuts, with no solutions.

This book follows *Another Way*, a 2024 volume of high school writers in Jefferson County, Texas, right next to Orange County. *Another Way* came after two dialogues among adults held at Lamar University in 2022 and 2023. All this focused on the extreme weather and inequality. We are also part of a made-in-Beaumont book vending machine project that gives books to middle school students to boost their literacy. Thank you to our friends and partners including Lamar University's Literary Press, Center for History and Culture of Southeast Texas and the Gulf Coast, Department of Sociology, Social Work and Criminal Justice, and Department of Curriculum and Instruction; the *Beaumont Enterprise*;the United Way of Beaumont and Northern Jefferson County; and the Beaumont Independent School District.

Ancient to the Future means taking responsibility for the future. So let's keep talking about these and other stubborn problems of daily living. As the anthropologist Margaret Mead famously said, "Never doubt that a small group of thoughtful, committed citizens can change the world. Indeed, it is the only thing that ever has."

Kate Williams
The Ancient to the Future Project
http://ancienttothefuture.org

Introduction

When I first began this project, I wanted to create something that would allow young writers across Orange County to share their stories. What emerged from that vision is more than a collection of student writing; it is a record of how a community of young people has come to understand resilience in an ever-changing world.

Students from Bridge City, Little Cypress-Mauriceville, Orangefield, Vidor, and West Orange high schools were invited to write about the ways extreme weather and inequality have shaped their lives, their communities, and the world beyond them. Some wrote about the storms they've lived through—the kind that tear apart homes and reshape landscapes. Others reflected on the quieter aftermath: the rebuilding, the adapting, the waiting for what comes next. Many recognized that the same forces that batter our region also reveal its strength and resilience.

What unites these voices is not only the shared geography of Orange County but a shared determination to speak. These students remind us that writing is both testimony and transformation, not just a means of expression, but a way of claiming space in a world that too often overlooks young voices. Writing allows us to name our experiences, to process what feels unspeakable, and (perhaps most of all) to make meaning out of chaos.

For these students, the act of writing becomes a way to resist erasure—to say, "we were here, we saw this, we felt this." It is, in its truest sense, a kind of protest: against indifference, against invisibility, and against the idea that only certain stories deserve to be told. Through writing, they transform private struggle into shared understanding, and in doing so, they remind us that language itself can be an act of resilience.

This project also grew from the vision of Kate Williams and *Ancient to the Future*, whose commitment to uplifting young voices has carried us through the entire process. Her organization's willingness to spend effort, time, and money has been an invaluable asset to the publication of *The Storm Inside*. Dr. Williams and *Ancient to the Future* understand that when young people write about the storms they've lived through—both the literal and the social—they're not only describing survival, but describing new ways of coming together to form a community of resilience and success through hard work and shared experience. *Ancient to the Future* has helped to transform the local realities of Orange and Jefferson counties into a collection of voices that speak to something much larger: the resilience of the youth and the enduring power of the written word.

The Storm Inside stands as a testament to what happens when we listen to the next generation. It is proof that their words can rebuild what storms have scattered; that stories can create bridges where divisions exist. Orange County has always been a place defined by its resilience. We've weathered storms both literal and figurative, rebuilt homes and schools, and found ways to begin again. The students in this anthology carry that same spirit forward through their writing.

These young writers are not only documenting the world around them—they are reshaping it. In a county where storms return year after year, their creativity becomes its own kind of shelter, proof that meaning can persist even in the aftermath.

Through their voices, we see a region that endures—not just through rebuilding what was lost, but through reimagining what can still be made.

—Allison Grace Harmon, Editor

Poetry

No New Beginnings
Takota Burnett, Orangefield High School

I had a flurry-haired friend
He enjoyed school, his parents, and math
Soon that enjoyment would come to an end
A hurricane made his house, his home, it's path
His family promptly moved after the news
After the disaster, there was nothing more to lose

The boy was now in a low, downgraded house
And the cold, uncomfortable floor he slept
His parents hold him so he won't rouse
In a nearby city another boy wept
He Heard the thunder and the pitter-patter
Though, in the warm comfort, nothing else did matter

He was oh so well off
Up there on a higher ground
He watched as water spewed into a trough
With this sight, he knew he was safe and sound
No worries, no destroyed buildings
All that, and no new beginnings

When a Bayou Storm Calls
Whitney Cunningham, Bridge City High School

In the quiet of August heat,
when the bayou holds its breath,
a whisper stirs the marshgrass
a storm has stirred from death.

She spins her skirt of seawater,
braids lightning in her hair,
and dances up from Gulf to pine,
with thunder in her stare.

The live oaks bend like bayou grass,
the roofs sigh, torn and tossed.
The frogs hush their nightly hymn
for all that might be lost.

But Texas folks, they board and brace,
with stories passed like rain
of Rita's howl and Harvey's tears,
and winds that call your name.

Still, morning finds the porchlight on,
a wooden swing upright.
The storm may break the levee's line,
but not the spirit's fight.

Dogs of Natural Disaster
Z Haley (Azriel), Vidor High School

Kicked to the streets,
cast out into the cold.
Stuck watching as the world around them depletes.
Their once soft souls, now resold.

As the water rises
and the storms grow louder,
the dogs of all different sizes
Are treated like a toxic talcum powder.

They've lost their lives
and were thrown from their homes.
Not a single one thrives.
All as lost as a bone within the catacombs.

They were tossed to the side when evacuations began.
It was thought to be in their interest.
When in reality, it was always the plan-
ditch the dog while all are distressed.

As a hurricane's water rolls in
or when the forest nearby catches aflame,
Dump the dumb dog who's as useless as a heterocercal fin.
Since a guilt free conscience was always your aim.

They walk around with bared fangs
and a broken growl.
It's sad to see how low their head hangs
all because your actions were foul.

You kick them aside when it got too cold.
They were deprived when the lightning would strike
Wrap your hands around their neck, staying in that chokehold.
Even that would be gentle then the way you've wrecked their psych.

Dog were made to be loved,
they crave a human's touch.

But when storms come up, to the streets they're shoved.
The cruelty of people will always be a bit too much..

I hope you get bit when their teeth clench down.
I pray for the day when the dogs get their way.
Because of you those dogs will soon begin to drown.
Millions of abandoned souls left to rot away in the rain.

Inequality Poem
Zoe Hunteman, Vidor High School

The waters rise with no abeyance.
Some find refuge, others drown in silence.
But who decides what homes stay,
And what homes are flushed away.
While some rebuild with ease,
Others search the wreckage for peace.

A Small Girls Life Float Away
Cambree LaComb, Bridge City High School

Walking out of school,
Backpack full of dreams,
She climbed into her mother's car,
Unaware of what the future might bring.

The sky was clear,
Not a cloud in sight,
They drove to the snow cone stand,
For her favorite creamsicle delight.

Later, lying in the house with the news on loud,
A shift in the air, a change in the crowd,
Overnight, her world was upended—
The storm was coming, fury unblended.

Tucked in her twin-size bed,
The winds howled, the storm spread,
The rain poured as the skies grew dark,
And her town was no longer the same mark.

From her window, her little eyes
Watched as the days passed by,
For four days straight, she saw the town she knew
Float away, leaving memories too.

Thank you, Hurricane, for the days with no end,
For this heartbreak she'd never mend.
The first time was cruel,
But to face it again and again was the real school.

Whether Weather Weathered Us

Jordan A Lowe, Vidor High School

Weather is big bad
It makes me very big sad
Inequality.

Water rising fast
The little house could not last
A family lost

I see all is lost
My sandwich burns to fine dust
I won't be the same

Lost in windswept night
Houses ruined like a blight
A dead man walking

The ground quakes beneath
A hellish pit splits below
Crashing, crumbling death

The storm is raging
A monsoon causes despair
Winds and water kill

The rumble of earth
A volcano's wrath explodes
Magma flying high

From under your feet
An earthquake in the dark deep
A tsunami lands

The ground washed away
From under the busy street
Sinkhole is opened

As I Look Around
Kelsey Matlage, West Orange-Stark High School

As I look around at all the storms surrounding me,
I breathe my air, unfair as it is.
I see people of all kinds holding signs,
Fighting for their rights in this kind of economy.
I breathe, feeling guilty that I won't breathe the same air they do.

I see the signs being waved, and people treated unfairly,
Shouting that they have rights—
Just like all of us.
As the storms grow bigger and bigger, no one seems to know
What kind of storm brews inside—not just in the climate, but in people.

As the climate worsens and the weather thickens,
No one seems to help those less fortunate than themselves.
We see them as beggars on the street,
But they're just trying to get by, like all of us.

You never know what someone is going through.
Unlike you and me, they've had to fight for their rights,
To be treated equally.
As I see the climate worsen and people grow weaker,
No one seems to remember that we are all people.

We are all human.
I look in the mirror, remembering what they taught me in school:
I might not have the same skin color,
But I know it's not fair to treat others unfairly
Because of their gender, their skin, or who they choose to be or love.

So I stand as a fighter, not a stranger,
Fighting for their rights along with my own.
As a woman, I know our climate may be getting worse,
But we still get to choose how we respond as people.

So we should stand as one

Instead of shouting and judging others based on how your life is,
Help—instead of turning away.
No one minds the rain until their umbrella is taken away.

Prey
Allison M. Parker, Vidor High School

Weather the devastator,
Destroying everything in its way like prey,
Praying for the lives they took away too soon,
The moon hides as the sun shines,
It is not brighter on the other side,
Gloomy and grey everything turned into its prey,
Empty shells as homes once stayed.

Like a Thief in the Night
Daphne Rabago, Little Cypress-Mauriceville High School

Like a thief in the night, Katrina took her rage out on NOLA.
Fists of wind
And a voice full of water.
Devastation already tore through the whole town.
Roofs torn from houses leaving them as islands while the cries for
help were afloat.

Maps marked red showing which neighborhoods are forgotten in
the rescue plan.
The one neighborhood that needed the most help and who showed
their NOLA pride.

Ninth Ward—
Black, poor, proud.
Waiting for the help they never received.
Left to be the body counted towards the lives lost.
Nobody took accountability.
The poor were left alone, scared, and helpless while the wealthy
received first class rescue.
Neglection killing so many that could've been saved.

The superdome—
Cots, people, sleeping bags, and trash scattered across the field,
the green was covered.
NOLA residents were seeking a 'safe' space, but it was really a
second storm.

The poor left for the streets with no luxury of evacuation.
Blamed for staying when they had nowhere else to go.
Buses gone.
Cars honking and lined bumper to bumper.
Streets crowded and water slowly creeping in.

Katrina ripped through without of care what your financial state
was.
Katrina didn't see color.
Recovery did.

White neighborhoods thought of first and rebuilt without retaliation.
While black neighborhoods are lost and forgotten because of discrimination.
While today the city is now retained.
The lives lost that day still remain the same.

Joy Comes in the Mourning
Lily Rendon, Vidor High School

The theology and deeper understanding of God has superseded all the injustices in my life.

In Genesis God said "Nation will rise against nation, and kingdom against kingdom. There will be earthquakes in various places, as well as famines. In Genesis 3:16 "These Are The Beginning Of Birth Pains."

In God's own words, he said the earth will quake at the pains of childbirth, because of our sin, the sin that has stained the earth.

From Cain and Abel came the first of the bloodshed. Death and destruction were never part of the plan.

In the beginning, God created the heavens and the earth, and in the beginning he looked at all of his creations and said, "It is Good."

But then, but then, the rivers gushed with the blood of humans and animals.

"What can wash away my sin?"

And yet, my lord and savior hung, beaten and bruised on a cross so that we could stop drawing blood. So that we could stop shedding blood, Jesus was tormented and beaten. His body lifted and hung on a cross for the final atoning sacrifice.

"Nothing but the blood of Jesus"

But now, my feeling of inequality is this.

These are the first of the birth pains.

Wildfires, animal sufferings, horrific deaths and hurricanes rule the earth and there is nothing we can do about that.

More deaths will come because of destructive behavior.

This earth is bound to me as I am bound to it.

The flesh will return to the dust from which it came, and the cycle will repeat itself.

Talking to Adam in Genesis, God said cursed is the ground because of You.

But I will make my plea, and I will cry out; God I know you hear ME!

Blessed is the ground because of you!

You gave your only-begotten son to die for our sins.

Blessed is the ground because it tasted of Your Blood.

Not mine.

Nothing But a Brick Wall
Landon Smith, Vidor High School

Sirens fire off. I feel the cool weather drain from my bright green yard. I see the beautiful color almost drain completely from my healthy lawn, the lawn I've made so many memories in. The red of the brick walls that hold the house up look as thin and as weak as a cardboard fortress. My hope fades away as I notice the worry on my fathers face. My stomach falls. My dad is the most calm I've ever seen one be, especially when it comes to emergencies. I close my eyes and pray for a miracle, but the wish was denied. My home, oh how I love my home. I see a wall of tears pool in the bottom of my eyes, I wipe them away. There is no hope anymore, just the means of survival. The race is on. The door slams close as we sprint to the shelter locked away in the basement. My sister and I hold each other as we cry together, hoping the only home we know, isn't ripped away from us. My ears pop, as the storm rocks my house, slamming the swing on the front porch, and throwing the old trash cans around, as if they weighed as much as a toy car. I hear the furniture being thrown around like ragdolls. Thuds are mixed in with the sound of a jet taking off are all that can be heard. When the unfair war ends, nothing is left, other than the brick wall with marks left on it from the years of measuring my height.

Lifeless
AJ Wise, Vidor High School

Pain paints paintings,
Some paintings are of the clearing once the storm has passed
Some, are murals of the devastation, painted along the canvases of
the victims
Walking with scars hidden under shirts and in the eyes that never
formed a tear,
You can tell a lot about the artist by what they choose to paint
The season of life they are going through,
We often walk through hurricane season
Trying to evacuate from the daunting task of survival,
Other seasons are filled with the scent of blooming flowers and
sunsets by the shore,
If the highs and lows of life were just a straight line
Much like a heart monitor, you´d be lifeless.

Fictional Prose

No One Came So I Did
Claire Fawcett, Vidor High School

It had rained for days. Everyone said it was just another storm, similar to the frequent showers we had gotten before, but this was different. It rained, pouring down on us for more days than I could keep track of. First, the ditches filled up with water. Then, once they couldn't hold any more, the streets flooded. Next, it came for us.

We watched the waterline rise, steadily coming up from the streets into our yard until it met the porch. Abuelita loved our porch. When her and Abuelo built this house, she made sure there was a porch. She hand painted it, and now the old paint was being damaged with the floodwater that was rising, further and further up. We lived in one of the lowest houses in the neighborhood, a similar height to the one next door, so before we could think of what to do, the water was inside.

We rushed to save what we could, piling things on high shelves and stacking them on top of furniture, praying that we could save what mattered. Abuelita was slowly collecting photos of Abuelo, not seeming to be in much of a rush, studying each one individually as if she thought they would disappear. Mama was trying to get her to hurry up, but Abuelita was even more stubborn than me, so there was no point. I looked out the window in our small house, trying to make sense of it all, when I saw that even the large houses across the street were starting to flood.

The rain had stopped, and I walked outside for the first time in two days. There was about a foot of water inside the house, and outside was even worse. Chairs, toys, and anything else that wasn't nailed down, flowed downhill in the river we used to call our street. Inside, we hadn't been able to save much, and it was heartbreaking. The house my Abuelita and Abuelo had made was ruined, and the memories inside were carried away with the running water. The constant waves from the rescue boats only made things worse. The boats sped by every day, picking up our neighbors across the street or the people who lived closer to the shelter. They always passed us up. The first day, my little sisters tried to signal them, screaming and waving, but there was no hope. They were too busy.

"Val!" I heard someone scream my name. I looked up and found my next-door neighbor, and best friend, Amalia waving from her roof.

"Ames!" I called over to her. "Is your family alright? We have stuff stacked up to sit on so we don't have to be in the water all the time. You know Abuelita couldn't get on the roof if she wanted to." Amalia laughed, her voice cracking with a mix of exhaustion and relief.

"Yeah, I think we're doing okay. Mama and I are trying to get Carmen to give up on rescuing her stuffed animals, but you know how four-year-olds feel about their toys." I smiled. Amalia and I had been best friends for as long as we could remember. Being the only two Latina girls our age, we clicked the moment Amalia moved into the house next to us. From the first day she showed up at my front door, we found comfort in each other's company. That porch had been our playground growing up, and now it was part of what we were losing.

"Dad has been stuck out of town for the whole storm, and because the power's out, we have no way of reaching him." Unlike my father, who had left when my sisters, Maria and Lucia, were babies, Amalia's dad lived with the rest of their family, but he often traveled for work. Because the storm was only supposed to last a couple days, he hadn't thought twice about going on another work trip, and now he couldn't help his family.

Mama called from inside the house, "Valeria, come here!" I called goodbye to Ames and made my way inside the house. "I just got word that they're opening the dams." Mama had been listening to her old radio ever since the storm had started, and thank goodness she had been.

The dams? Wouldn't that just cause more flooding? Our house was already drowning, and I didn't think it could handle much more.

"It's raining again!" I heard Maria and Lucia exclaim as they ran through the flooded kitchen. "I thought it would be over for good this time," stated Maria. "But I saw the rain come back," countered Lucia.

More rain was not good. If it rained more, in addition to the opened dams, the whole house could be underwater. I had to do something. Waiting around for a rescue boat wasn't working. The boats hadn't stopped for us. Not once did they even look in our direction. They had passed so many times, picking up neighbors across the street who had big houses and fancy cars. Never us. I couldn't rely on anyone else to save us. We were going to save ourselves.

We were loading up the makeshift raft when the water from the dam finally came. By now it was pouring again and we just needed to get out of here. Mama, the twins, and I were ready, but Abuelita was being as stubborn as ever. I looked at her again, as she clutched the photos she cherished, as if time itself was slowing down just for her. Mama was packing last minute food and essentials on the raft and rushing everyone out, but Abuelita would not leave. She didn't seem to notice the water creeping up, ready to destroy the photos she held onto as memories of her life. I felt a sudden rush of panic. We couldn't stay here. We had to leave. Now.

I waded through the water, out to the raft. Amalia and her mom were ready with their own raft, and Amalia was tying them together. Then a scream split through the pouring rain.

We all looked up to find the roof of Amalia's house was starting to cave in from the water damage, and Carmen on top, holding onto the railing with all her strength. Her face was pale, and she was trapped.

"Carmen!" I shouted. "Don't move! Stay there! I'm coming!" I started to swim over to the house, but then it hit me. Abuelita. I couldn't leave her. She was still inside, lost in her thoughts, unaware of the danger that was coming for her. I looked at Mama, her eyes filled with worry, and with my own tear-filled eyes, I knew what I had to do.

"I'll be back. I promise," I whispered to her, trying to maintain the fear in my shaking voice. "Just keep Abuelita safe."

I swam through the chest high water, struggling against the current, my focus only on Carmen. I couldn't think about the swirling debris under and around me, or the rescue boats that should have prevented this; I could only think about one thing: saving Carmen. When I got to the house, it was more unstable than mine.

I acted fast. It felt almost as if a group of guardian angels was helping to hold the roof up. It stayed when I climbed the chipped, wooden pillar to get up to the roof. It stayed when I crawled on my hands and knees from one end of the roof to the other, and it stayed as I got to Carmen and held onto her like she was my own sister. That's when it fell. As if in slow motion, I threw Carmen into the waiting arms of Amalia below in the water. Then I jumped. Everything went silent. I couldn't hear the screams of my sisters as the whole house tumbled into the water, or the cries of Amalia's mother. It was all quiet. I didn't know where I was. All I saw was darkness. It was almost peaceful. For a moment, I felt still and relaxed for the first time since the rain had started. But almost as fast as it had happened, I came up from the water, gasping and coughing for air. I looked around and saw Amalia and Carmen swimming towards me, and my mom swimming even faster.

"Mija!" I heard Mama's voice first, breaking the silence. "Mija, you're safe." I hugged her, tears forming behind my eyes. I looked around with my blurry vision, and to my relief I saw Abuelita holding a box of photos sitting on the raft, with Lucia and Maria on either side of her. We swam as fast as we could through the water towards the raft. The storm was finally slowing. Rescue boats would be coming again soon, but we weren't waiting around anymore. No one came, so I did.

The Unseen Wound
Bailey Gorham, Little Cypress-Mauriceville High School

As the thunder strikes and the rain pours, the breath I once had in my lungs has quickly disappeared. I attempt to reach out, but I find myself paralyzed in fear as the water surrounds me. One more step I tell myself, hoping and praying that the fresh air flows into my lungs like it once did so little ago. As I reach the surface, I believe for only a moment that everything shall be fine, that in just a few days I shall return to that place where memories have been placed and drowned beneath the depths of the waves that take over my childhood home, but as days shortly turned into weeks I find myself longing to be in the comforts of my home once again. When the parts of me that was left had at last returned home, I came to realize that childhood home I once desired to return to has but all perished to the ground, the same as wood turns into ashes in a fire. Everything that once was is now nothing, leaving me to pick up what is left and run as far as possible. I move forward, telling myself how utterly unfair it is to live a life like this one. Forced to be seen as the kid who faced the flood, the kid who couldn't find the tears to cry after such a tragic suffering, the kid left to question everything moving forward. If only the ditches were deeper, I tell myself, if only we had the resources of money to rebuild what was torn away like all of those that surround me. Then at least I could find myself with a slither of hope left inside me, then for a moment, I could pretend it was all but a bad dream, but instead, I face the graving pain left inside me that of which scars me with a wound deeper than the eye can detect, leaving me broken and lost, picking up the pieces of the past and carrying the burden of memories moving toward the future. Alone, quietly, and without a trace of happiness in a world surrounded in pain and misery. I get through it, but at a patronizing cost that only I shall ever see.

The Pale Castle
Desmond P. Gross, Vidor High School

The wind blew a breeze that was all too familiar to Eriklov. It was the same as in the balloon a few days prior. It was the breeze of a storm coming on the horizon. In all his life using the balloon, he had never seen a storm such as this. He tried to forget about the wind, for he would only worry about it and stray from his mission.

Eriklov strode up the steep brick pathway that led to the Pale Castle. It was so high up from the village that he felt he could trek the trail for hours and never come across the same stone twice. He knew, however, this would not stop him from reaching the top.

As he went on, the chords of a pipe organ hummed in the air, ever growing. The sound of the music was enough to frighten any man from taking a step further. That was the whole purpose of the Pale Castle owning an organ in the first place. Still, it wouldn't make Eriklov turn back. He had never failed a mission before. Today would not be the day it would happen.

The road went forever on and on. The storm was coming fast, he had been climbing the steps and stones for hours, and he was running out of breath. Sheer will of man and determination was why Eriklov kept going. He looked west and saw the dark clouds beginning to engulf the mountains miles and miles away.

"I shouldn't have put this off so long," he thought to himself. "I should have known Bella could have handled the village." No matter how often these thoughts entered his mind, he would not let them consume him. The roles he had to play changed a man. Nothing could stray Eriklov from protecting his people. So he trekked on, and on, and on.

Another wind gusted along the path, putting Eriklov off balance only for a second and blew his long, golden hair in his face. When he regained stability, he brushed his hair behind him and looked up to the Pale Castle looming over him.

He had just realized it had become night when he looked up. The moon's rays beamed from beyond the castle's tall and twisted spires. Its stone was as pale as the moon itself, and the roof's tiling was a very contrasting shade of black. It was almost a beautiful sight, if not for who Eriklov knew was in the castle's chambers. But even with that knowledge, he just stared. The organ was loud now. That alone told him he was close. When one chord played, bats from the Pale Castle's many chimneys and towers flew off and squeaked in the night sky. Even a terrified man knew he couldn't go back now.

Eriklov felt a strange feeling of entrancement towards the castle, as if it was beckoning him. However, if it was asking him to leave or to step further, he was not entirely certain. He didn't know what to do at this point, as if his motives had completely left him.

Not a single person ever made it this far to the castle without running back to the village in fear. Or at least not any person who lived, that is. Some have told ghost stories of a spell that drew those too close to the Pale Castle to draw even nearer and never return. Eriklov never knew that those stories had a truth to them. As much as his mind was telling him not to draw nearer, he knew in his soul that he had to.

Each step he took towards the castle felt more and more dreadful, as he had to push his will against his mind just to make it to the door. His instincts and hope clashed, but his determination finally broke through. As soon as it did, he found himself at the black ironclad door. There were two giant knockers that were clenched in what resembled a bat's jaws.

Even with the fearlessness he possessed, Eriklov's heart sank, the chords of the organ ringing in his ears and through his head. He caught hold of himself and gained the courage to knock at the door. As he lifted the knocker, the sound of rust squealed from it. He knocked three times. As soon as he finished, he heard the echo of the knocking menacingly growing further and further away. Just as threatening as the echo, the deafening organ suddenly stopped. It was completely silent.

A few moments later, he heard footsteps from beyond the door, growing ever closer and louder. As soon as he heard the loudest step, they stopped, and he heard chains rattling past the door and many locks clicking open.

Then the door swung open, revealing a tall, skinny man who was almost as pale as the castle he resided in. He had noble black and red puffy clothing. Eriklov had seen this man only in drawings around the village. This was Lord Alveron. Even though Eriklov tended to the village, this was the man the people worshiped. Eriklov hated him. Lord Alveron and his castle of subjects were the fearmongers of the whole village. The Lord stared deep with his blood red eyes into Eriklov.

"What is it you man-thing wants from the residents of the Pale Castle?" he asked with a soft, yet snarling voice. Even though he felt dishonorable doing so, Eriklov knelt and bowed to the Lord. It was the only way he would win over the Lord's almost nonexistent gratitude.

Eriklov spoke as steady as he could, holding back all of his fear. "Lord Alveron, I come to ask you if you would spare some room for the village to stay." Lord Alveron curled an eyebrow and kept his stern expression. Eriklov stayed kneeling, as if speaking to the floor. "There is a terrible storm coming that will flood the village. The only safe place that is high enough is here at the Pale Castle. Will you please let us in? We are only asking for shelter, no bedding and no food. Please consider us."

The Lord stared at him for a moment and began to erupt in laughter. Through the laughter, Eriklov looked up and saw a pair of fangs glistening in the moonlight behind the Lord's lips. Eriklov began to stand, but Lord Alveron stopped his laughter and with a stern voice spoke, "Keep kneeling, mortal, if you know what's best for you."

Eriklov's blood began to boil. He had never felt such anger from words before. Not only did he not kneel again, but he shot up and stared Lord Alveron in the eye.

"I will not kneel to someone with no honor and respect such as you. I will never kneel to the man who terrorizes our village with no intention of helping us," Eriklov proclaimed. The Lord looked disgusted down at him. "Use this time now to change your ways. I will ask again. May we enter your home?"

The Lord looked down upon him. He showed his fangs through his lips and snarled.

"I will not open my home to a village of ungrateful scum who don't know any better. I give your village all they need and more, and they send an unloyal man to ask for more. You humans are so pathetic. We are so much better than all of you, I'm offended you'd even think that we would share rooms and food with you. To your question, I say no. Good day," the Lord said, very strictly.

"Go to hell," yelled Eriklov with all his might.

"I will never go to hell, mortal. It seems though, after this storm, you will be there yourself," he said. Eriklov could see how little the Lord truly cared through his eyes. Then the Lord spoke one final saying, "Good. Day."

The door shut in Eriklov's face, and he heard the chains once more and the locks clicking back in place. Eriklov saw himself in the small reflective spots on the iron door. He felt ashamed. He let his anger get the best of him. These thoughts echoed in his mind to the point where he had a migraine. "I failed," he said to himself, his voice almost whimpering. He failed.

The storm was drawing ever nearer. The wind rushed, and the organ began once again. Eriklov banged on the door with his bare

38

fists as loudly as he could. There was no answer. The storm began soon after. Through dirt, wind, and rain, he banged on the door over and over again, never stopping. He wasn't going to let the storm stop him from his goal.

Human will and determination were something the Lord and his Counts would never understand. Even after they shoveled Eriklov's molded and dirtied corpse from a puddle of mud and water when the storm was over, they never understood the equality they had.

When the Waters Rise
Adison James, Vidor High School

I was only a young girl when the storm rolled in that ruined my life. This is a retelling of that dreadful morning.

A sudden crack jerked me from my sleep. I groggily pulled myself from the warm shelter of my blankets, looking out the window and being met with a view of the small tree in our front yard being pulled to the ground from the force of the whipping winds, the rain pelting the glass like a frantic tapping, as if the water was begging to be let in. Even though it felt like I stared at the window forever, it was only a moment before my mother burst through the door. The panic across her face was evident as she held my small brother in her arms. She looked around the room before frantically grabbing my school bag and dumping it on the floor. I opened my mouth to ask what was going on, but I felt frozen in place, waiting for her to tell me what to do. She silently rifled through my small two-drawer dresser and shoved clothes into my bag before turning to me with a soft yet tense smile.

"Genny, baby, I need you to grab your rabbit and your shoes and wait for me by your door, okay?"

I held my stuffed rabbit in my lap as I pulled on my pink sneakers, running my fingers along the hearts on the velcro straps as I secured them. I hopped off the bed, walking to my bedroom door. I looked back to my mother as she shoved the folder with all our important paperwork haphazardly into the bag. She then swiftly turned and moved straight past me in a daze, out into the small hallway, reaching up for the attic cord. She pulled it down, the old springs and wood cracking and creaking as the ladder unfolded. My mother pushed me towards the ladder, urging me to climb up. I grabbed onto the ladder, dodging the few broken rungs, and climbed until I pulled myself into the attic.

As I waited for her to climb up, my curiosity felt as though it was boiling over, and I finally blurted out, "Mom, what's happening? I'm scared." My voice, sounding smaller than ever, barely carried over the howling of the rain. My mother quickly set my brother down on an old pillow and came to me, cradling my face in her hands as she always had when I was frightened, and told me in a voice that sounded so sure it felt as though she could stop the storm herself with just her words, "It's just a storm, baby. We're just going to stay here until everything passes."

I nodded, nuzzling my face into her hand. They were rough from years of working two jobs and taking care of us, but they were a reminder that she would do anything to protect and provide for us. I reminded myself this was no different—she wouldn't let anything happen to us. My mom slowly pulled her hands away, stood, and brushed the dust from the attic off her pants before quickly moving to cover the windows with the spare boards we had lying on the floor. I pulled my brother into my lap, gently rocking him as I watched my mother move swiftly, making sure the winds couldn't break the windows.

Once she made sure everything was secure, she went to the trunk that gets tucked in the back of the attic during the summer months, full of the blankets we can't use because even the nights are too hot for anything more than the worn, thin cotton sheet to be on you. She pulled the blankets out, making a pallet on the floor. The blankets, not much thicker than a sheet, provided little to no padding for us to lay on, but it was better than risking splinters sleeping on the bare unfinished wood. She laid the pillows she had grabbed along with the bag on her way up on one side of the pallet, making a makeshift bed. Then she gently grabbed my brother from my arms and laid him down, tucking him in under his small blanket he always carried with him—a tattered little thing, but it brought him comfort.

As she finished, she reached out to me, pulling me into her lap, and she just held me. It was like she could sense my fear without me having to say it. She moved my hair from my face and said softly, "Get some sleep, bug. I'm sure the storm will be gone when you wake up." I nodded, my eyes slowly closing as sleep took me into its arms.

It couldn't have been even two hours later when we heard what could only be compared to a bomb going off in the distance. We could feel the ground beneath us tremble ever so slightly. I sprung straight up, my brother next to me erupting into shrill cries after being pulled from his sleep by the noise. My mother swiftly scooped him up into her arms and rushed to the window, pulling away the boards she had laid against them, trying to crane her neck to see what was happening outside. She wasn't able to see much at the moment, but we could hear a faint sound of moving water.

Though she couldn't see it, my mother knew what was happening. She had read the papers in the weeks prior about the leaks in the levee—about the weak spots they were working on fixing—but they procrastinated. The levee remained looming over our small city. My mother suddenly paled, silently placed the board back over the windows, and walked back over to the pallet. She crouched down in front of me, holding my hands, her words seemingly caught in her throat. She sighed and said to me, "Genny, I'm going to be honest with you because you're old enough to understand what's happening."

The fearful look on her face told me everything. I felt my throat close with fear, but I simply nodded for her to continue. "There is a flood coming, and I think it might be coming right to us. I just want you to be ready." She gave my hands a firm squeeze as she finished talking, and all I could manage was another weak nod.

The distant noise of running water now felt more like a herd of horses running their way through the streets, trampling whatever got in their way. Below us, we could hear the water collide with the siding of our house. We could hear the creaking of the window pane as the water pressed its way in. We could hear my brother's cries mixing with the screeching winds, and I could hear my mother praying under her breath for God to save us.

My mother unclasped her hands and went to pick up my brother, pushing him into my arms before rushing back over to the windows. She pulled away the boards with more fervor than before, then looked around at her feet before stooping down to grab a hammer from the makeshift toolbox in the corner. Holding the hammer firmly in her hands, she brought it above her head and swung it down through the window, smashing the glass and the thin wooden frame that adorned it. She tore off a piece of her dress and wrapped it around her hand before frantically pulling the glass from the frame. The feeling of the rain hitting her skin and the glass slicing it open was indecipherable.

She finally got it to where she could grab a blanket and throw it over the bottom of the frame. She turned to us, grabbing my little brother from my arms and gripping my shoulders firmly. "Genny, the water is here, and I'm going to need you to be brave and help me get you and your brother onto the roof before the water can rise any farther." I know my face must have been as pale as a ghost, but I just nodded.

My mother gently grabbed my shoulder, guiding me to the window sill. "I need you to climb out onto the roof and wait for me to hand your brother and the supplies out to you. I can't carry them all and climb at the same time." Looking from her to the slowing winds outside, I knew I had to do this for her—a seemingly simple sacrifice in the eyes of all she's done for us.

I began to push myself upward, my mother's hands lifting me the rest of the way. She instructed me as I climbed to shimmy onto the flatter area of the roof and wait for her to hand something out of the window. She called my name, and her hand appeared with my book bag, stuffed full with the blankets and toys we had brought to the attic. I quickly grabbed it from her, placing it behind me on the roof.

"Mom, I'm ready for you to hand me him." I could hear my mother whispering a soft prayer as she picked him up into her arms and handed him out of the window to me. I scooped him quickly into my arms, cradling him tighter than ever before. My mother quickly followed suit, climbing out of the attic. It felt as though, as her foot hit the roof, the shattering of the living room glass rang out below as the water rushed in, signaling that we had moved just in time.

We looked out around us at the houses being swallowed by water in the distance. All we could feel was hopelessness. We made our blankets into an SOS signal, hoping one of the rich people with boats might help us, but we knew we had no choice but to wait.

The Freeze in Bainbridge
Oliver Kershaw, Vidor High School

Georgia is often known for its peaches, possibly even 'southern hospitality.' One thing it's never been known for, however, is snow. In fact, snow was a remarkable rarity in Georgia, with only 6 recorded instances in hisa 5 day annual average. While the town occasionally caught a hint of winter frost, any real snow was nearly unheard of.

The beginning of this tragedy, it was a normal day. Well, normal for the South anyways. There was a bite that was quite familiar lingering in the air, the kind that made the locals shrug, grab their jackets, and move on with their day. That particular winter had already thrown a few cold spells their way, but the weather reports for the day made it sound like just another routine drop in temperatures. As usual, the news stations, weather apps, and social media were abuzz, with messages advising residents to bundle up and prepare for a "chilly" day ahead. But as far as anyone could tell, it was just another southern winter, where temperatures dipped just low enough to make everyone uncomfortable but never enough to rouse a real concern.

"Don't worry folks, no freeze, just a breeze!" the newscasters on every channel claimed proudly, their bright smiles framed by cheery graphics. The phrase was comforting, almost laughable to anyone who had lived through a dozen mild winters in the South. People knew to prepare for a cold wind that might make it feel colder than it was, but no one could have imagined that what was about to unfold would be anything close to the kind of weather that would make anyone actually afraid.

Temperatures were reported to not go below the mid-60s that night, however when the sun set, an unfamiliar chill crept up all of the town folks' spines. People went about their routines. Parents picked up their kids from school, and families made their way home from work, the chill nipping at their skin, but still no sense of danger in the air. The evening passed as it always did, with the slow lull of southern evenings. Even as the sun disappeared completely, the temperatures seemed only to sink a little lower, but everyone brushed it off as just another winter night. Aer all, it was a cool evening in February.

However, that sense of calm quickly unraveled. By 9:00 PM, the forecast had already proven to be a bad joke. The temperature was now dipping toward 40°F, a quick drop that no one expected.

inherited some of the older houses were the first to know this chill. This cold was different. It was harsh, intrusive. It was the cold that began to slowly eat away at you, from the inside out.

In many of the homes that dotted Bainbridge's older neighborhoods, the heating systems were built for milder winters. These homes, usually passed down inherited through family tragedies, had charm. They had character, even if they were never really meant to withstand the kind of cold that was now overtaking the town. Old houses- with their hardwood floors, creaky windows, and insulation that might have worked fine in the 1940 snow felt like ice boxes.

Those who owned them oen did so because it was all they could afford. The ones who lived within these monuments were considered unfortunate in Bainbridge. Yes, these older houses were alluring, but they always had a price. To own one of these houses, they had to be inherited. The only way to inherit them from stingy ancestors was from a loss. These people obtained houses from relatives who passed from natural causes or unavoidable tragedies. There were even conspiracies that some of them poisoned their family for it. Remodeling was a complete waste of a thought. It was way out of everyone's budgets, and most of these homes had fireplaces that no longer functioned properly, or their chimneys were clogged with years of soot.

People in Bainbridge, especially those living in the older parts of town, weren't used to this kind of weather. They're houses weren't very insulated and they could just never get used to the nibble on their cheeks and noses of the frosty air. They could easily go to the local hardware store and buy gloves or space heaters, but in many cases, they just didn't have the money to keep up. And the ones who could afford it were few and far between.

By the time midnight rolled around, the temperature had dropped into the 20s, and a bitterly arctic wind whipped through the trees, carrying with it a promise that things were about to get much worse. News channels had started reporting about the unusual and unpredicted cold spell, but by now, it was too late for anyone to really prepare. The frost had begun to paint the windows of many homes with an icy texture, the kind of ice that you couldn't just wipe away with a handkerchief or use your breath to melt away. It clung to the glass as a reminder that this wasn't just a bothersome night, but something much worse.

As the temperature continued to drop, it began to snow. At first, it was just a dusting, a light flurry that some people could have easily written off. But by 3:00 AM, the snow had accumulated at an alarming rate. Roads that were once clear now shimmered with a thin layer of ice. Vehicles that were le outside—old cars, cheap cars—were now encased in frozen layers of snow and ice, their tires stuck in place. It was clear that Bainbridge was in trouble. This was no light dusting; it was the kind of storm that made roads impassable, the kind of weather that crippled even the most prepared towns in the North.

But within the city limits of Bainbridge, not one person was prepared. As the snow continued falling and the cold kept settling lower, more and more families started to realize just how vulnerable they were. Even the wealthy, who could afford to take a break from work or head out of town, were not immune to the resentful freeze that was taking hold. The town's power grid, old and barely able to keep up with the heat of a summer day, began to fail, freezing into darkness. Blackouts started to sweep through the town, homes plunged into darkness, leaving families cold and isolated.

The ones who were fortunate enough to live in the newer areas of the town were mostly safe, with their insulation in the walls and under the floors, the heaters blasting warmth around the home. They were the lucky ones, the ones who didn't have to bundle up under layers of blankets or rely on candlelight to navigate through the darkness of the begrudging night. But even they couldn't ignore the cries for help from the others, the ones stuck in the older parts of town, where homes were crumbling, where families couldn't afford space heaters or emergency services.

In the early hours of the morning, the temperature reached an unthinkable 18°F—far below freezing. Emergency services, stretched thin, couldn't get to everyone. The wealthy residents who could afford to escape to hotels or seek shelter with friends in other areas were doing so. But for the rest of Bainbridge, there was no escape. This storm wasn't just a natural disaster—it was an indictment of the inequality that ran through the town's very foundation.

People who had been living paycheck to paycheck were now staring at frozen pipes, cracked windows, and the desperate hope that the power would return before they ran out of firewood. And as much as everyone tried to stay positive, to maintain that southern charm and optimism, the truth was undeniable: people were cold, desperate, and scared.

Bainbridge was not the only town in despair, but in this small corner of the South, where snow was a devastating stranger and freezing temperatures were more rare than water in the desert, the storm revealed something much deeper than weather. It exposed the gap between those who had a financial net to fall into and those who did not have anything to catch them, the disparity between the ones who had the means to weather the storm and those who could barely keep their homes warm.

As the hours dragged on, with the snow still falling and the cold creeping in, the town could only wait and hope. Those who were suffering the most, the ones without proper heating or financial security, could only hold onto the hope that the storm would pass. But the real tragedy was that the storm wasn't the only thing they had to face. In a town where the poorest were left to fend for themselves, it seemed that the cold was only the beginning of their struggle.

The Dividing Eye
Logan Odom, Little Cypress-Mauriceville High School

Hurricane Anima wasn't what destroyed this town; the people did. The hurricane had an eye, but it could not see.

The people had eyes, and they chose not to see.

"No tip" was written at the bottom of every single check, despite Demarcus's efforts. He rushed out of the kitchen, carefully balancing six steaming bowls on a dented metal tray. He shifted to the side as a coworker walked past, unmoved and unbothered. Demarcus dashed to the table. "Three mushroom soups," he said, handing them out. "Two vegetable soups," he placed them gently. "And one chicken noodle," he added, lowering it in front of a kid in a letter jacket.

The kid was an Englewood Eagle. It was ironic that the school chose the mascot, not because they were fierce predators, but because eagles looked down on everyone else.

Demarcus lingered for a second, as if expecting a thank-you that wasn't coming. He was met only with the sounds of slurping. He tucked the tray under his arm and speed-walked toward the kitchen, muttering under his breath: "Rabbit stew, extra cheese... French onion soup..." He repeated the order like a mantra.

"No tip," the family of six had offered. Their table was deserted now, but they hadn't been shy about leaving a mess.

The sun finally went down as Demarcus washed the last few plates. He flicked the water off his hands and stopped to admire his work. Then, he turned and headed for the back door, wiping his hands on his pants. He stepped outside and felt the first raindrops tap his shoulders. The sky had been holding its breath all day. He unlocked the door to his hand-me-down Ford Pinto and climbed in, just as the wind started to pick up.

It was pouring down and thundering as Demarcus pulled up to the trailer. He ran to the door, rainwater at his ankles. He took his hat off and threw it onto the floor. "Ma, I'm home," he said, walking to their bedroom. "Ma," he said, opening the door, excited to tell her about his day.

She lay on the bed in her clothes, her wheelchair by the side. She was asleep. Demarcus quickly flipped off the light switch, sighed, closed the door, and walked to the living room. He went and sat on the couch and stared up at the ceiling. They used to have a TV, and he missed the days when he and his mother would sit and laugh at game shows and sitcoms.

Thunder crashed outside, and the power went out. It wasn't much different from when the power was on, anyway. Demarcus accepted that there was nothing else for him to do today, so he took a shower and got into the only bed with his mother.

Demarcus woke up, his head pounding. Everything was uncomfortable. He was disoriented, damp, and confused. He groaned, opened his eyes, and stared at the sky through the window. Confused, he sat up, looked forward, and saw carpet. They were lying on the wall. The pillows and blankets floated past him as the smell of murky water filled his nose. Demarcus's eyes went wide, and he tried to stand up. The trailer swayed, and he was knocked back down to the floor. "Ma!" he said, crawling over to her and shaking her.

She mumbled, turning away. "Lemme sleep."

"Get up, Ma, our home is flooding!"

She opened her eyes and addressed the situation. Then gasped and reached out for him. He grabbed under her neck and legs, lifting her up. He stumbled as he stood. "What happened?" She asked, clinging to him. "I don't know," He stumbled, walking through the living room and to the front door. With one arm, he held his poor mother, and with the other, he reached up to open the front door. He lifted her up, setting her through the door and onto the side of their house, now facing the sky that put them in this situation. He then climbed up too. They stared out into what was once the trailer park, now not much discernible from a lake. Broken pieces of trailers floated by like dead fish.

Demarcus called out for help, but the rain drowned out his cries. "We're gonna be okay, Ma," he said, hugging her. "We don't... we don't got no insurance," she said, voice thin. "Where we gonna go now?"

Demarcus avoided the question because he knew the answer, and he didn't like it. He huddled in close to his mother, and they waited for the storm to end or for someone to save them. Hours went by, and the storm showed no signs of stopping. The rain poured for three days. When it stopped, Demarcus was asleep on the top of the trailer. He was awoken by the sound of an engine. He sprang up and, in the distance, saw a boat with two men on it. "Hey!" he stood up and yelled. "Over here!" The men looked over at him, but continued going straight. "We don't have any room!" One of the men yelled. "We'll come back, okay?" Demarcus could feel his heartbeat in his throat as he watched them drive away. "Okay!" he shouted, and they didn't look back this time.

"Ma, we're saved!" he said, spinning around and grinning. "Ma?" he spun around in a circle, looking at the entire surface of the trailer. She was gone. "Ma!" he whirled around, scanning the water. The trailer had drifted far away from where they had started. She was paralyzed from the waist down. He knew that she was gone.

He began to hyperventilate and sat down. He rubbed the sweat off his face and tried to calm himself. Maybe she was okay, somehow. Maybe a boat found her. He stopped and prayed for what felt like the millionth time. Now, he just needed to wait for that boat to come back and save him. Demarcus waited for over a day; the boat never came back.

He lay on the top of the trailer, wishing that it would be over. He was hungry, he was cold, and he was weak. He stared up at the grey sky as tears rolled down his cheeks. He was hopeless. Then, something else caught his eye. A house, right next to him. He turned his head and saw rows of houses. He had drifted into Englewood. He stood up on the trailer and scanned the houses frantically for some hope of rescue, when he saw something. On one of the roofs of one of the houses, there was a family of six. The very same one from the diner. They were huddled together, and their house had collapsed. He yelled loud enough that the littlest boy heard and pointed, tugging on his mom's skirt. Damarcus motioned for them to come forward, and one by one, they swam to the trailer and sat on top of it. They sat there for one more day, and when they woke up, the water was down to their ankles. Demarcus helped them off the trailer. FEMA flooded the town, eager news reporters right behind them.

***

A week had passed since the hurricane started. "My name is Rebecca Robins, and I am here in Englewood, Texas, where Hurricane Anima hit. We're here with Kaleb Mutt, a survivor of this category five disaster. How did you and your family survive?"

"Well," he said into the microphone, "We made it on the roof and thought, 'This is it.' Then, a guy on a trailer floated by and we tagged along."

Demarcus sat on the curb, watching all of the families get food. But they were only for people from Englewood, there was nothing for him here. "Mark, right?" Rebecca walked up, stuffing the microphone in his face.

He flinched back before looking at her. "Uh, Demarcus." He answered timidly.

"And tell us, Mark, how did you survive?"

"Well, after a boat abandoned us, I sat on the top of my trailer for five days until the water went down. I lost my home. I lost my mama. I don't got nothing left."

Rebecca turned away from him and toward the camera. "As you can see, many people were affected by this catastrophe," she buzzed, walking away.

Demarcus sat, staring, when someone approached him. His boss, from the soup kitchen. "Hey, Demarcus, glad to see you're alive!" He said, patting him on the shoulder. "Hey, Mr. Harvey," he forced a smile. "Hey, I need you to come into work Monday, alright?" he asked.

Demarcus bit his lip and looked down. "Roger that, Mr. Harvey. I'll be there." And his boss turned and walked back to Englewood. Demarcus stared at the people as they laughed and ate; he was stuck in a world that chose not to see him. He was divided from everyone else, not by the eye of the hurricane but by the eyes of the people.

Bad Weather

Alexis Simmons, Vidor High School

The weather is all the poor girl could hear, the ripping and howling of the earth falling down to nothing but rubble. Oh how the feeling of the howling winds wrapped around her like a blanket of insecurity and chaos around her. If only the world could stay together to keep the girl safe, to feel at home and not scared of the world around her. If only mommy and daddy could hold her in their arms again.

The girl screamed, hiding under her bed shivering and shaking as the booms came louder and louder, more violent, more aggressive. She could hear it from just outside her room, outside the door. Her safe haven was slowly being crushed by the loud booms and harsh winds threatening to rip apart her world into nothing but rubble. After a life changing storm, could anyone truly feel happy? She thought this was a silly thought and that this weather would grow quiet as if it were a soft, tranquil river flowing. So it was happy in her tiny world, in her small slice of peace, but without warning the river became violent and angry, ripping away at the earth, at the banks, dragging branches down the river to turbulent waters, drowning any sense of joy or peace in its wake.

Over and over the girl saw the raging storm and saw the aftermath of the tough turbulence.

Black and blue, yellow, green. That was all the little girl saw on her mommy's skin and eventually on her own skin, being dragged into the eye of the storm, the centerpiece of hell.

To have to be in the eye! All she wanted to do was hide in her hole in the earth in a safe house away from the thrashing storms, the blowing winds, and the wounds of the hail. The little girl did her best to run and escape from the eye of the storm, to find her way back to her room, the safe place, her safe place, so she could live in her space hiding under her bed where the bad weather could not reach.

She went from hiding from the storm, hiding from the world and then was thrown into the eye for hours on end locked outside in the storm as the hurricane came full force booming, slashing as the water on the bays reached the homes of others, as the lightning hit all around the little girl. All she could do was scream and cry and feel the sting, the pain. It hurt, it really hurt. Why did she have to hurt so much? Mommy, Daddy, please?

The little girl had finally made it into her room, locking the door behind her, shaking and shivering, gripping her skin, pulling on the flesh. Her world was spinning. Her world was flipped. Why must she be hurting from the storm while others didn't even get rain, not a drop? So dry, just like the barren Sahara desert. She was just so sad. She made sure the storm couldn't get into her safe place before she hid back under her bed and covered her ears with the palm of her hands. She was safe. The little girl sniffled, her tears starting to settle down. She no longer felt scared as the storm passed for today.

What Made Up for the Lost Years
Justin So, Vidor High School

Four days at sea. Four days. A harsh voice. "You're gonna get off the boat." I walk off the plank. Limping on to Chinese soil. I feel like I have worms in my stomach. That black sky. Shielding this world from happiness. Doesn't need the yellow sun's help. Food is something I need, badly. What would my family think if they saw me in my state? Especially hurt if they he-twak. Life, blurred? I hear people, laughing? Why is my head hurti-oh. A wall, in front of me, a bustling market behind it. Pain. Pain. A darkening world. A paper to me. No. Why am I not allowed to stay? Wait, no, no, stop. The light returned. I grab onto a rough tree. Don't crush the caterpillar.

A noise? Oh, a rat, famished. How cute. Oh, a yellow cat, what a cute phoenix crown. Oh, a fat, top hat cat is coming too. Oh, oh. They are fighting over the kill. The poor rat was just trying to live its life, happy, like... the people in these walls. "Please, give some food to the poor," "You must have heard of the flood, show some piety, show your silver." Hands on the ear. Think they might use it for opium. Can't give out my last worth. Don't burn a hole in my pocket, dollar. I pushed my legs. An infinite line of beggars. They sit with destituteness next to them. Faster. Why must you growl my insides?

The shops are everywhere now. What made people stop. How tired are my legs? The shopkeepers are also stopping, and starting to. "Oh, God, bless these poor souls with your kindness and love." A preacher. He towers and white that perfectly reflects light. How much does he pay his cleaner? Must 400 silver. They don't care though. Bowls in hand, some line in front of the soup pot already. Fatter people, fatter than people here, seem to listen intently. The people around me glare, but defeatedly walk past. I snub my nose, though, truthly want to crane my head down. I follow the crowd.

The dark sky, I am drawn to it. I stopped, however, as did many others. I follow the darkness towards a speaker, "People of China, we must fight these foreign oppressors." Did he just throw down a pot? "We are the greatest and we have done this dance many times, we will win!" Does that include the Manchus? Don't say that, the answer is clear. I feel what the people around me are thinking. "Yes, those Christian are evil," "Wealthy China under the boot," "Foreign allies will die." I feel the glares as I walk away, but I must, I won't be a part of such evil.

I walk, trying to not be noticed. Yet as I hear, some people don't feel the same. "7 silver, that is insane, I just got here and haven't even made one." "Well, that isn't my problem, if you can't pay I'l..." I sat down on the side, I felt I should watch this and my legs hurt from walking. "Please sir, I just came from Northern China, you have heard of the flooding of the Yellow River, have pity." The man just shook his head and started motioning the guard next to him to arrest the man. Then a few people, who were walking nearby, started coming, a white sun on their armbands. "How dare you Qing dare rob us, we will destroy you." They started grabbing chairs the store owner owned and beating the official and the guard. Splinters flew, hitting them and even all the way to me, I just took it. Silver also flew, but none flew to me, the people of the white sun took it all. Another person, seeing this, came too. "How dare you beat that poor official and his guard." A foreign man. Familiar? He started beating the people, umm, all of them, taking all the money. More people seeing this came too, wanting the money only, people in military uniform, having a red star, or with a more foreign look. The store owner looked like he could just die there, while the official... I left, sitting had made my stomach more hungry than standing, it was hard to stand.

Ugg, my stomach is killing me. Is the world spinning? Green turns to blue. An orderly world disorganized and crushed before me. The world is turning. My hands are just screaming. Bodies piling before me. The caterpillar died. By me? No, no. I must run away, run away, head stop hurting. Please?

Food? "Would you like food sir." A man in red? No, that must be his allegiance. I should get my money. There... my ticket, letter of deportation, and an American dollar, within me. "I will take that, sir" He looks so happy. I want this... "Oh, umm, hey sir, why are you leaving. Didn't you say you were hungry?"

Run. Run. Run. Run. I must run away from it all. The screams, death, the chains. I must... my stomach. Why legs, why, are you failing me. My house! My house! Over there. I must get over there! Run, run to that opulent palace of rotting wood and a small field of rice.

My mother and father, inside the room of only natural light from the bright yellow sun. They're reading the letter... I must stand tall, I must, must be the strong one before my crying mother and father, yes, yes. My legs, they are failing, it can't be. Mother and father, you don't need to embrace me. I am not crying. The world,

55

it is dissipating into colors, twists, runs, blues, and darkness, it embraces me.

I am starving. I am starving. Rice, my fields? Yet I am starving. Dark sky, yellow sun, and a world of darkness. I reach out my hand. Hey, why are you taking my rice? Hey stop that person in a black belt. Wait, no he has a rifle, a foreigner, someone that looks somewhat like me, no they look very like me, they aren't one. He is a man in military uniform. He has a white star? A red star! Yes. Wait, why do I care about his allegiance? He is just taking my rice. I am starving. I am lying. The sun. The bright green sun is shining. It feels nice actually. It is blinding me.

Walls, colorless, surround me. From my perierview, my mother and father. They are looking at me. They are pushing something at me, crying and yelling. It is a pile of sunflower seeds. I look at the seeds and then them. Why must I struggle through such a hard life. How am I supposed to live? Mother and father, what if the future is so dark, that death is a mercy.

Yet as I felt the green sun over my body, I felt hope. I look at the sunflower seeds yet again. I slowly move my hand up and grab the sunflower seeds.

It seems time has stopped when I grabbed the sunflower seeds. Then, green came pouring out of my hand. They wrapped my hand. Bright, yellow sunflowers bloomed. The darkness that surrounds me seems to be burned away. As I stared at the sunflowers, hope seemed to blossom within me and I flew.

The world, once again came to. Wrinkled hands, a plush chair are the first to reach my eyes. Then a desk, a drawing of my mother and father and a picture of me and my family next to me, 1980 on it. On the other side, a bowl lay. My head swiveled and eyed a child. The child stood pulling a curtain to shower light into a dimly lit room. "Grandpa, you awoke," "Yes, haha, I did." The child came closer to me. "Grandpa, mother told me that when I was born, you told her that it made the eighty-nine years worth it, could you tell me what you meant." I looked at her weakly, her eyes clear as the sky. I took the food out of the bowl, and put it into her hand. "Here child, some sunflower seeds to eat, as I tell you about the lost years."

Personal Narratives

Untitled

Jannath Bhojani , Little Cypress-Mauriceville High School

Staring at my watch while my teacher rambled on about trigonometry, it felt like just another normal day. The bell rang, and I headed home. I ate dinner, then sat down to watch TV until a public safety announcement caught my eye. "Flood warning in effect." I shrugged it off, thinking it wouldn't be anything serious, and went to bed. Little did I know that would be the night my life would change forever.

The next day at school, the buzz was everywhere. "I'm going to Dallas!" my best friend shouted excitedly. I smiled weakly, knowing we couldn't afford to go anywhere. I watched everyone make plans to leave, while I stayed quiet, dreading the storm I could already feel approaching.

The rain started, and soon it wasn't just the sound of drops hitting the ground—it was a roar, relentless and deafening. That night, I hugged my younger siblings, trying to comfort them with words I didn't even believe myself. "Everything is gonna be alright," I told them, but the truth was, I was terrified.

As the night dragged on, I checked my phone. A photo popped up on my best friend's Snapchat story: "Finally in Dallas!" She looked so carefree, posing in front of a skyscraper, like nothing was wrong. Another friend posted, "No school today! Feeling so lucky!" My fingers trembled as I scrolled, seeing their smiles, their excitement, while I sat there, waiting for the storm to swallow me whole.

And then I heard it—the drip, drip, drip. My heart sank. I rushed to find the leak, feeling the water drip down my bedroom wall. I panicked, but somehow managed to grab a bucket and place it under the leak. As the night wore on, I moved more buckets to collect the water leaking through the ceiling. My chest tightened with every drop, every second that passed.

By the time the storm passed, I was exhausted. My house was flooded with leaks, no power, no food, and no way to fix it. But we had no choice but to stay there, huddled together, because we couldn't afford a hotel room. I saw my friends post photos of their safe, dry homes, while my family was stuck counting every last dollar. My friends' parents were getting checks from their insurance companies, while we were still trying to figure out how to patch a broken roof that we couldn't afford to repair. Even the disaster relief people were slow to come, as if we were forgotten.

Weeks passed, and things didn't get better. Every time I walked past the house, I saw new homes being rebuilt, fresh coats of paint, luxury remodels—all for the families with money. But for us, the damage remained. My siblings and I had to sleep in the same wet rooms, our belongings still damaged and scattered. Meanwhile, I watched the world move on, while we were still drowning—in water, in debt, and in the crushing reality of inequality.

In the end, I learned that some storms don't just destroy your house. They tear apart your chances for recovery. And while the world moves on to rebuild, people like me are left to pick up the pieces, over and over again, with no real help.

Sadly, this is the harsh truth for many people I've witnessed in Southeast Texas. This story is based on real experiences—not just my own, but the struggles of my closest friends, neighbors, and family. Fortunately, I never experienced the worst of it, but while I saw privileged friends adding glamorous remodels to their homes, my family couldn't even afford to repair ours. It's a painful reality, where the wealthy can move on and rebuild without hesitation, while those with less are left behind, struggling to put their lives back together with no help.

Extreme Weather
Peyton Doucet, Bridge City High School

My name is Peyton Doucet, I am a senior at Bridge City High School and I plan on attending Stephen F. Austin University this upcoming fall semester. January 24, 2023, at around 4:30 in the afternoon, a tornado hit Bridge City, Texas, ruining my home, belongings, and my mental health.

January 24, 2023, started out like an ordinary day, I woke up, brushed my teeth and showered, and then got ready for the day. Me, my mom, and all three of my brothers ate lunch at a Mexican restaurant while my dad was at work. We were eating and Keaton, my oldest brother, started talking about how he was going to a friend's house after we got back home from eating, leaving just me, my mom, and my two other younger brothers at the house later that day. When we got home from eating, I went to the gym by myself to get a quick workout for the day, and when I returned home I was tired, so I decided I wanted to take a quick power nap. As I got into my cozy bed, I was scrolling through my phone before I closed my eyes, but before I could get there, everything started feeling unusual.

I start feeling this weird pressure feeling in my ears that I have never felt before. I tried not to think much of it, so I decided to go downstairs and grab some water, just hoping the feeling in my ears would go away. As I walked out of my room, I looked out the window in front of the staircase, and I saw a big ball of grey, dark wind, spiraling toward me and my house. Before I can even react, my window busts open and a log of wood comes flying through as well. Terrified, I hide behind the wall as I am panicking. All I could think about was, "Am I about to die? Is this really the end?" As I am hiding behind the wall, I hear my mom yell from downstairs, "Peyton get down here in the closet, hurry up!" After I heard this, I ran as fast as I ever have before to get to the closet. As I am running down the stairs, another window busts open! I knew I couldn't stop and hide like I did earlier, so I decided to just keep on pushing until I got to the closet. After what felt like forever, I made it to the closet, where my mom and two younger siblings were there, all of them looking terrified. When I got in I tried calling my dad, but my cellular service stopped working before I could explain to him what had happened.

After the tornado had passed, we exited the closet and took our first look at what the house looked like. There was glass and debris everywhere, the big wooden log, and water also got in the house. We went outside and saw trees had fallen everywhere, and the outside looked dark and nasty in general. Our garage door was busted into the garage, our shop building was completely destroyed, and our chicken coup was blown over, but the chickens were okay! After we regathered ourselves after the crazy weather, me and my mom started cleaning up everything we could. My dad and my brother came home as soon as they heard the news and helped too. After doing everything we could, I had to sleep with wood for windows, no electricity, and nightmares from what had just happened.

This was the most traumatic experience I have ever gone through. It took months for our whole house and yard to finally be back together, but to this day when the wind starts blowing hard outside, I get scared and nervous. That tornado will always stay in my mind because of how much it changed my life, all for the worse. I am so grateful that I had the family and friends to help me through the tornado, but I will never forget how much trauma it has caused me. If anyone ever goes through something like this, stay strong! The trauma is definitely hard to get through, but with Jesus Christ, prayers, and family, you can get through anything.

No Calm Before the Storm
Jaylin Hock, Bridge City High School

I sat nervously in bed, listening to the rain pour outside, the darkness around me fading as the light from my TV illuminated the room. I squinted my eyes and checked the time. Sighing, I laid back and tried to distract myself from the anxiety creeping into my gut. I had seen the news; Hurricane Harvey was not a new subject for me. Just a few hours ago, my Dad had driven me to my Mom's house in the storm, then he went back to salvage what he could from our home. I had been waiting for any news from my Dad about what he could save, but I was only nine years old, and with no phone I had to rely on my Mom to pass me any messages.

After listening to the wind rush past my window for too long and watching videos to distract myself for a few hours, my Mom finally came into my room with her phone. It was my Dad on the other end of the line, and I was too hopeful that everything would be okay. The storm outside turned into muffled background noise as I talked to him on the call, and that was the first time I had ever heard my Dad cry. There were four words he used that crushed any of the hope I held tight to, "Our house is gone". After he hung up I couldn't hold back my tears either as I thought about the things he told me. He had to race against the water inching up to the roadways and wasn't able to save much. However, he reiterated that the most important thing was that he and I were safe, and he told me he was going to stay with his friend Tim.

To The Believers and Unbelievers Alike
Lily Rendon, Vidor High School

A retelling of my freshman year in high school, on March 21, 2020, the day a tornado made landfall in Vidor, Texas. A whirlwind of destruction sought new grounds as I sat in a hard, blue chair in my "boring" fourth period class, staring off, listening to the clock's persistent ticking. *Tick, tick, tick.*

Not knowing a wretched disaster was brewing, my classmates and I stood still in utter shock, when we heard the roars of thunder. And like the beginnings of a war cry; thump, thump, thump, you could hear the thud of our hearts beating in unison. The lightning was so bright we were all like little deer caught in the headlights of a poacher, petrified and overwhelmed. *Tick, tick, tick.*

"Alright class, listen up" my teacher said as he fixed his posture. He sternly started to explain the situation that had put our lives in danger. But, it was as if I was held down, struck by the lightning itself. My mind was too shocked to process what he said. The only demand I heard from his native speech was "Okay class, line up, single file." obeying my Sergeant, I trooped behind fellow classmates to our designated area. *Tick, tick, tick.*

I watched the atmosphere shift before my eyes, Tick. The teachers paced back and forth, yelling for our names and shining flashlights at us...*Tick, tick, tick.*

"Name?" An older woman demanded with a wild sense of urgency, as she lifted a clipboard and pen up to her chest. *Tick... thump, thump, thump.*

"Lily Rendon," I blurted out nervously

"Thank you." She said, in a rushed voice.

Tick... Not long after the interrogation, the buzzing of the teachers came to a halt, after another heart-pounding noise. *Ba Boom!* Jarring lightning lit the dark hallways, and my body was now curled up and pressed against the lockers. I tried to hide from the forces of nature that prowled just outside the double doors. *Tick, tick, tick.*

Uninvited cold wind waltzed in with bad manners, leaving me and my classmates drenched. *Tap, tap, tap*, the rain's rapid intensity broke the silenced hallway. *Bam!* The door slammed shut.

Even though this storm wasn't bloodthirsty, many other storms have taken innocent lives. And for me now, four years later, I am closer to the people that I love more than ever. It seems unimaginable to not understand the danger I faced, while being in a high school environment. However, in my walk with Jesus, I have realized facing a literal storm, and facing internal conflict, is much the same as enduring the chaos of a natural disaster. This analogy reminds me that sometimes, when we are experiencing the chaos of life, we can make cozy places like our homes look blissful when we are still in a whirlwind of destruction. I look back and wonder what the faculty had to do that day, and I considered the students at risk. ch the same as enduring the chaos of a natural disaster.

The responsibility and conundrum of adulting weighs on my mind as I think about a "funny" video a past schoolmate made during the storm. The short film consists of him outside in the hateful weather, acting like a meteorologist. He said there was a "good chance of rain"....viewing this as a kid with no responsibility, I didn't comprehend the danger he was in. But, I tried to imagine watching this video in an administrative position. If he got hurt, who would be liable?... The storm?... The school?... Him? These questions opened up a whole new adult view.

What do families do when FEMA withholds help, and the city officials they rely on let them down? Were the city officials at fault for culvert failures during Hurricane Imelda? How do you suc the city for your own house not being high enough or strong enough to withstand flooding? Its not FEMA's fault because they didn't help me, us. but so many people need help from FEMA. Are the taxes our family pay to the city and the government not a proper investment? Is this the consequence of a simple vote. Well, maybe insurance will help, right? These are some of the questions I personally had to face when considering inequality and accountability concerning liabilities.

I didn't get FEMA help after Harvey, and my house was in shambles, years after the storm. As a young child, I couldn't help but wonder about the people who did get financial compensation. My mom would say encouragingly, "Don't be embarrassed, we are God's girls." and at the time, I didn't understand this statement. I mean, who is truly liable for years of embarrassment and dirty socks when I simply walked to the kitchen...me?

Destruction comes, and we stand firm in our ideologies. We trudge the battlefield hand in hand to fix what was broken. We select the "right" politician, and suddenly we are the little women, marching towards natural disasters, armed in galliance. But, how many times do we do this until justice is served?How many times are we going to be subjected to not having proper help? This is how I feel about the government, and morality, concerning the right way to take action, against injustice, when having to rebuild homes time and time again.

> We The People
> Are we, the People.
> This ideal is constantly slipping through the fingers of a person
> so vigorous to grasp it.
> How can I see clearly through a tainted window?
> The bile is served on a platter branded U.S.A.
> A delusional mindset that disguised itself as a yearning for justice.
> We the people made ourselves judge over right and wrong.
> We The People deny the concept of morality.
> We the people have already repeatedly constructed broken homes.
> I am tired of piecing together this city of rubble.
> And am tired of continually being shown up by "equality" and "justice."
> We are not the people.
> We did not make these rules.

This poem gives me the sense that the notions surrounding the words "inequality" and "injustice" are the reflection of the false narratives we have all fallen victim to when thinking the government would be a consistent, reliable source. But, there are holes in any human construct, because that's what it is, a human construct. The government, charities, churches and people do there part. But, we do our part, we have to.

From these various questions, this verse from Matthew 5:48 gives me an answer, "for He makes His sun rise on the evil and on the good, and sends rain on the just and the unjust". This verse resolved my idea that there could be an unfair God.

Regarding the feelings of hopelessness, when home-wrecking weather destroys everything you have. You might feel like there is no help when piecing back together the city of rubble left behind. But, I will show you, through my own cut variation of Mary Evelyn Williams' poem,

"It's just a good thing", that even though I didn't get help from FEMA and the storm ravaged my home, God is the only true source of equality. "He rains on the just and the unjust."

"It's just a good thing . . . GOD above has never gone on strike . . . Because HE wasn't treated fair, or things HE didn't like . . . Do you know that God will be Justified? . . . For no one has ever been more abused or treated with disdain than GOD, And yet, . . .With all the favors of HIS GRACE . . . Men/Women say they want a better deal, And on strike they go, But what a deal we've given GOD, to whom everything we owe . . ."

In 2nd Timothy 2:13, it says, "If we are faithless, he remains faithful, for he cannot disown himself." Likewise, God can not disown himself, because he is his attributes. His actions will never be unrighteous, they will always be justified. This serves as solid evidence when, in Ecclesiastes 3:11, it says, "For there is a time, for every purpose under heaven." There is a time we will face another storm, whether that be spiritual or physical. Jesus says in John 16:33 "I have told you these things so that you may have peace. In this world you will have trouble. But take heart, I have overcome the world."

Matthew 7:27," Those who follow Jesus' teaching are like a wise man who built a house on a rock. Those who ignore Him are like a foolish man who built a house on sand. (your spiritual house) One will survive the violent storm. The other will fall hard. (We face the same storm, but we arent all in same boat.Genesis 7:1-24) The same is true of those who face the storms of life." (present day) You can adorn the outside of your home with whatever political standpoint and ideologies, but, if the foundation of what you live your life by is not true, it will not sustain when storms come. Mark 4:35-41 Jesus commands the storm. "Be quiet, be still". The government can only do so much. We the people who make up each individual community in each State, in each city and in each zone can only do so much. Churches and charity can only do so much.

Nature + Man Vs. Woman
Miley Rice, Vidor High School

I've seen my house get destroyed and rebuilt twice- once by nature, and once by a system who leaves its hard working people behind. I've knocked sheetrock out of its frame, ripped up soggy flooring, and painted bland colors onto new walls twice- failing to hide the deep scars left behind. Knocking, ripping, and painting, Knocking, ripping, and painting.

The first time was due to an unavoidable natural disaster. But the second time was a choice. An unforgivable choice proposed by governing bodies who don't care about the people who suffer the most tragic life of being impoverished. The pools of tears and sweat that could have caused a flood on its own wasn't enough. The rich and powerful decided the people at the bottom of the food chain have to suffer one more time.

Hurricane Harvey was meant to be a once-in-a-lifetime event. It was a struggle that everyone felt but persevered, unless you were poor. While the rich people fixed and cleaned their ditches, repaired their culverts, and even got flood insurance, the less fortunate held on to the lying statement "once-in-a-lifetime" event; a lie echoed by news outlets and those in higher social classes. It was as if the well-off and media conspired so that the less fortunate were unprepared for the second war against Mother Nature. They hid the truth to protect themselves, hoping to see the poor scramble like hopeless, headless chickens one more time.

When you're poor, you can't afford the "just in case" precautions. So maybe if you were loud enough, the city would listen and fix the things you couldn't afford. But why would they invest in the neighborhoods that don't offer "potential growth?" So the life you lost and rebuilt just two years ago flooded again from another hurricane because you were too poor and your voice was too quiet. So, if you have no money and no voice, take out a loan, a federal loan to help those affected by extreme weather. A loan that will keep you from retirement. An interest rate that will keep you in a house you dread to come home to because it reminds you of your worst fears. A number so high you realize you are stuck in that old smelly car that drives you around a town that doesn't care about you. A loan that reminds you everyday that maybe if you worked a little harder, stayed in school a little longer, you could have the money to get out. But instead, the hard-working people with inadequate salaries get poorer, and the rich- cold and unwavering- ruthlessly get richer.

My Mother was a victim of this cruel system. She was a beautiful southern magnolia tree uprooted by hurricanes and tipped over by bodies above her. I didn't understand this as a child, but as I grew older I realized that my youthful innocence shielded me from a life of tragedy that you can't escape unless you have wealth or influence. Though, this shield didn't last long. My mother has given me everything I could dream of while all of her dreams slipped through her fingers. The carless governments and punctual monthly loan payments curse this life onto her, day by day.

So every day I think about the things I could have done to protect my mom from this relentless world. How could I have been a little smarter, more resourceful, and more hardworking during the lowest points of our lives. What 10- and 13- year- old me could have done to help my mom escape the downwards ramp titled "quality of life". Would she be happier now if I wasn't so worried about losing my favorite outfits and collection of stuffed animals back then? Guilt fills my skin, lungs, and heart every time I think back to both hurricanes.

Instead, I think about what I can do to help her in the present and future. I imagine becoming a lawyer or a doctor-any high earning career to pay off her loans and mortgage, buy her a new fancy car that would drive her into a new city, a new life. Maybe even an extravagant house on a foreign beach, a place she's only dreamed of, a place she's never seen. I've always wanted to become a teacher, but I couldn't let my selfishness get in the way of making my mom's dream of comfortability come true. She has given me the freedom to pursue any future I desire. How could I turn my back on her now? I can't leave her living paycheck to paycheck until she is too old to work for a system that has no regard for her. I can't leave her with the inescapable truth of bankruptcies and no retirement, all while chasing a path that could very well lead to the same fate.

All these worries would vanish if we had more- more money, more power. The linear path of struggle and guilt would fade just if we had more; more everything. Natural disasters leave ugly scars on the poor while rich people slip away with nothing but a papercut. No matter how hard or fast you try to climb the ladder to a better life, hefty price tags will drag you down every single time, back to the life that no more than fortunate creature has to experience. The harder you fight the life caused by natural disasters, the deeper you sink into a tar pit of inequality.

Weather's Toll on My Life
Brooklyn Richardson, Vidor High School

There have been things that have impacted my life, good and bad, but one thing that doesn't come to mind when thinking about memories is the impact the weather has played on my life. I have been extremely fortunate to experience very different weather stories that many of the kids around me haven't. I grew up in Virginia, and from a young age, the worst stories of weather came from snow. There would be blankets of thick, white, fluffy snow that wouldn't be there when we closed our eyes at night, but in the morning, it would be the only thing you could see.

In 2018, I moved to Texas, where snow wasn't the thing that would cause school to close. Buckets of water would fall from the sky, sending the town into extreme chaos. Shelves in the stores would be bare, sandbags would be handed out, and the families that were evacuating would be in a hurry to get out and get home. This was all new to me. Why would there be so much worry about some water? In a short amount of time, I would soon be a victim of losing a home to weather.

When the water entered my house early in the morning, the lights in the house all turned on in a hurry. "Everything off the floor that you want to keep, Brook. Try and do it quickly," my stepmom quietly said to me as my bedroom light came on. I did a quick overview of my room. There were clothes scattered everywhere—some clean, some dirty—but no real way to tell the difference. My school bag was half unzipped and the unfinished schoolwork stacked on top. Hot hair tools were thrown on my floor. "I'm now understanding the importance of cleaning my room," I mumbled to myself as I threw my hair in a quick updo and got to work.

I started scooping up all of my belongings and stacking them on my bed. As I picked up a box of pictures that captured memories from throughout the years of my life, my dad walked in to help me. I could see the worry painted all over his face.

"Dad, we will be okay." I tried to comfort him, but I'm not sure how successful I was. At 12 years old, I really didn't understand the severity of what was about to happen.

"Brook, you can't just stack things on the bed. Pick the most important things you want to keep and stack them on your shelf," my father said in a very annoyed tone. I knew he didn't mean it to be rude or brush me off like he did.

"Yes, sir." I quickly got all the things that held a lot of meaning to me and stacked them on the top of the shelf. He had built this for me when we first moved into this house to store my things, but I, like many kids my age, would rather use the space on the floor.

Soon, the whole family was just sitting in the living room, and all the things we needed to do to prepare had been taken care of. We filled buckets with water, got everything off the ground, and did the best we could to put sandbags out where the water had yet to come in. As the day started to come around, we silently watched the water enter our house, slowly watching all the things we loved get ruined. It started invading the house from the garage, which my parents had turned into their room about a year ago. Within a short period, we had watched about three inches of water take over. My dad sometimes broke the silence with small comments of, "During Harvey we didn't get any water," or, "The damn city of Vidor needs to get it together."

I gathered from his comments that my dad's house was in the "safe zone" during Hurricane Harvey. My grandparents, cousins, aunts, uncles, and all of their furry friends had come here because they lost their homes to the storm. We were the only home in my family that was untouched. Now all the roles were switched. During Tropical Storm Imelda, my home was taken. As I watched all the things I loved slowly get ripped from me, I didn't understand—why my house? This was a tropical storm. We should have been just like the ones around us, untouched. But this was not how it was.

As we left our home to find a safer space to reside until the storm passed, I got to look at the homes in the other parts of town. Some were unbothered, others looked like mine, and some looked even worse.

Little did I know that this would all become permanent imprints in my memory. But this wasn't the end of all the chaos.

As the rain drained off, we entered our home for the first time since we left. The water left a horrid smell, stains from where it had landed on the wall, and some of our belongings were unusable.

Within hours, the studs in my house were exposed, floors torn up, and all the furniture that we could no longer use was thrown in a pile outside by the road. Everyone in my family had come to help. My house wasn't the only one that looked this way. As I looked down the road, as far as I could see there were piles. All the things my family had worked so hard to accumulate were all thrown away due to water. I couldn't wrap my head around how all these things could be taken away from us so fast.

I remember having a conversation with my older cousin who had come over to help. He could see the worry all over my face and reassured me that these things happen, and that it would all go back to normal with time. This wasn't true. FEMA didn't help. The memories from this storm didn't just stop after my house got ripped into pieces. It never got put back together. Sheetrock was screwed up on the walls to hide the wires, the floor was still concrete, there were no covers over the outlets, and piles of tile lay in my yard until the day we moved out.

Even though I'm older, the imprint of how poor my family was continues to stick with me. Of course, at the time I just thought that my dad was lazy and didn't care that we lived this way. I was embarrassed about the way my house looked. All the kids around me at school had their houses back, and the storm didn't still affect them years later. I was too young to understand that the kids around me were more blessed than I was.

With time, I learned that the city was the cause of my house taking in water. After Harvey, the culverts were redone to fix the flow of water. While the effort was made, it wasn't executed in all parts of the city. The parts that were home to poorer people were not taken care of the same as the rich side of town. My home should have never been taken from me during a small tropical storm, but due to the city's efforts—or lack thereof—to maintain a fair living environment, I lost my home.

Losing my home at a young age was a traumatic event, but it has brought great things and aspects to my life. I didn't learn to appreciate things more, have patience, make great connections with people from the community, and many more valuable things, all on my own. I owe a big thank you to Tropical Storm Imelda.

Harvey Hit Hard
AJ Wise, Vidor High School

My siblings and cousins were all swimming in our ditch. I hate getting dirty, but we have no power. Using a small lamp as the only light we can use, so I took a hard pass on the shower. I'm the oldest out of all of my siblings in my family, and that's saying something because I'm only eleven years old.

"AJ, want to go sliding?" my dad asked me.

He explained to me that we had pool floaties that we could use like sleds and slide down our neighbor's hill. We only had one float, so my siblings counted me down from across the street.

"One, Two, Three," they all yelled in unison.

I ran as fast as possible on the hill that had a small layer of water on it, and dove in. I slid past the road, which kind of hurt, and splashed everyone.

They squealed and we danced as we took turns sliding and splashing.

After I was tired of playing, I went inside looking for my parents.

"Dad! Dad! Dad! Hey, Amber, where did Dad go?" I asked my step-mom.

I never called her mom. She's been in my life since I was 2 years old. She is more of a mom than my real mom, although I feel some kind of loyalty towards my real mom that makes it feel wrong to call her mom, too. As if it would betray her in some way.

"Dad went on a fourwheeler with Mr. Craig to the store. All the roads are flooded so they are riding on the railroad tracks to get groceries for us."

"Wait, the bald guy? We don't have any fourwheelers either." I was confused. My dad wasn't a "country" kind of guy. I began to giggle at the thought of my dad bouncing up and down in a fourwheeler.

"Mr. Craig has four wheelers. Neighbors take care of each other," she said, smiling as if she was grateful towards me. I also found this funny, considering my parents don't like everyone. Now they are suddenly best friends with Mr. Craig.

"Okay." I ran off and got some chalk and started to go to work. I decided our sidewalk was too sidewalky.

I drew rainbows with sheep jumping on it. I tried to draw the Playstation logo, but I couldn't remember the way it looked. As I was drawing I got carried away and used my entire chalk in hand and played with its shavings around like sand.

A loud roar came from down the road. I looked over with

chalk in my hair and on my arms. I may or may not have used the shavings as war paint.

"Dad!" I ran to my dad as he hopped off the fourwheeler with a lot of bags in hand.

"Hey bud." He gave me a small smile.

I followed him into the neighbor's house and I laid inside their house for a long time. They had two dogs. One was black and white, while the other one was white with brown. The white one had the prettiest eyes that were bluer than the sky.

I wish dogs could understand me. I keep trying to stare into his eyes but he keeps moving.

He squirmed around as I bugged him. He eventually got tired of me and left, so I just laid on their carpet.

Their living room was so cool. It has stairs that go down to a separate section by their fireplace. The wood pillars were so cool too! I never would have thought of making a house like this. Wait, I wonder how you make a house?

Eventually some lady called for me. It kind of made me feel bad. She knew my name and we had been neighbors for 8 years, but I didn't know hers.

I went into her kitchen and she had all kinds of food on the counter like homemade granola bars and some other food that I didn't pay attention to. I was too busy slobbering all over the tasty treats in front of me.

"Eat as much as you'd like!" she said cheerfully.

If Amber says it's rude to eat all their food I'll tell her she said it was okay. I'll probably be in trouble anyway, but I don't care right now. The food is way too good to care about that!

I went to bed that night dreaming about the granola bars.

We woke up and everyone hopped into Amber's car to charge our phones. I felt like the coolest kid all the time because I've had a phone since I was 7. Most people would find that absurd, but my parents got it for me for protection. My real mom's house could be scary sometimes.

I didn't like to tell everyone I had a phone. Well, that's a lie. I told everyone who thought they were cool for having one I've had mine longer. Although, I didn't play it much and didn't rub it in people's faces.

While Amber and Dad were scrolling on Facebook like old people, I used my fingers to open my mouth as wide as possible and put it in front of the car vent. I liked the feeling of a dry mouth.

Soon, it would get old and I would drink some water, but I would miss the feeling so fast. I ended up just repeating that process a few times until my parents turned off the car.

I really missed AC, more than I thought. It's not something you really realize is good until you don't have it. Amber said a lot of things are like that. My dad said to enjoy what you have because it won't always stay the same. Not sure who's more right, but it is something I do think about.

Following that, my parents moved the cars into our neighbor's driveway and grabbed some chalk and wrote in big, bold letters, "Food, Water, and BEER!" My dad thought it was funny. I thought it was funny because his forearms were orange afterward. We all giggled, stepping back and looking at our work.

"Maybe a helicopter will come and give us supplies," Amber said cheerfully.

"Maybe they'll give us beer," my dad and uncle both said at the same time.

I got all the gumballs—small spiky balls that fall off trees—in our yard and played dodgeball. Our game got interrupted by a military truck. The tires of it were the same height from where our roof starts. The bed of the truck had a cover and women with babies were inside of it.

The next day we used the fourwheelers to go as far down our road as possible. We got down the main road that leads to all the stores, but it was flooded. We were watching one of the really big trucks go through it, and its tires were devoured by the water. It had water touching its doors. As the truck slowly got out of the water, we saw that it was twice as tall as the one we saw the day before. My dad said it had to be 13 ft. tall.

Picking our jaws off of the floor, we all hooped in this man's boat. It was so thin I was sure we would sink. We got through about 2 football fields and we got in someone's vehicle.

Riding around the town I saw cars floating down the ditches with trees following suit. I saw some roads with only chimneys.

"Amber, where'd their house go?"

"I'm sure it is just hiding," she said smiling faintly.

Dad said some houses hide just when it rains. Our house never hides. It stands strong in the rain and wind, poking its chest out, showing its shiny star on the front.

"Our house isn't scared. It never hides," I said, poking my chest out too.

"Some houses can't be brave."

We were silent the rest of the ride, watching as neighborhoods were completely gone. Highways looked like they were low because of the high water. There were no people out on the street like normal. I wonder what happened to them? Harvey has introduced me to a lot of new people. Not people I would choose to be around, but it has been fun meeting everyone.

"Help us pick up!" Amber yelled at me. My parents said we had to help clean up my uncle's house. I didn't like getting dirty, even though our shower was normal again.

They showed me the inside of the house and I decided helping them wasn't so bad. About 3 ft tall all around their house was torn out walls, and the floors were all concrete, suddenly missing their vibrant wooden flooring.

It's not that all the houses were hiding. Just not all of them weren't strong enough to stand.

Extreme Weather and Its Relation to Inequality
Karely Zuniga, West Orange-Stark High School

I was about nine or ten years old when Hurricane Harvey hit, and I lived in Port Arthur, Texas in a single parent home with no support from anyone financially. The storm struck us hard and forced us to evacuate to higher ground. With no option, we spent what was meant to be a singular night— that later turned into a month and a half—with a family friend who also had children and was affected in the storm. Not only have our two mothers worked through emotional and financial stress to put food on the table, pay rent, and buy necessities, but they worked night shifts just to afford basic needs. They did all they could do to ensure that my brother and I were protected from the effects of the hurricane. They worked hard to give us two a level of comfort and safety. Our home had been destroyed. What would we do now? Where would we go? In a city that was being destroyed in every direction it was clear that our lives had changed and we weren't the only ones affected by it.

Natural disasters like Hurricane Harvey hit low income communities the hardest. They bring new levels of poverty and amp up existing levels of poverty. Low income communities usually exist in flood prone, poorly constructed housing with flexibility in neighborhoods, if or when disasters hit, they may likely lose everything without insurance, savings or community to step in as support. Climate change is contributing to greater severity and frequency of storms, flooding, and heat waves. Climate change worsens cycles of poverty in existing vulnerable communities plagued by systemic injustices and inequities.

There is also a racial dimension to this crisis where Black and Brown people are often more impacted because they live in systemic inequities like redlining, education funding disparities, wage challenges, and less generational wealth. Decades of housing discrimination displaced families to flood prone neighborhoods with crumbling infrastructure. Environmental racism compounds this risk as community exposures to pollution and industrial hazards are worsened by climate events that negatively impact health, both during and after. When assistance finally arrives, it often is delayed, inadequate, or is not accessible to those who do not have the resources or social capital to navigate the bureaucratic maze. Black New Orleanians after Hurricane Katrina waited longer for FEMA assistance than their white counterparts. The same happened after Harvey. These failures do not just hamper recovery—they make it virtually impossible.

I believe that the intersection of climate change and poverty is one of the greatest injustices of our time. The communities that contribute the least to environmental degradation and inequity suffer the most and have the least resources to build back. After Harvey, I and families like mine were left abandoned to restart with little assistance and surge in housing costs and structural barriers to recovery. The impact of having everything taken included the trauma of loss, economic insecurity, and emotional strain that does not simply and magically go away once the flood waters recede. Children in these most vulnerable communities now face education gaps, food insecurity, and emotional trauma and strain that change their future opportunities. Meanwhile, those responsible for the climate crisis, because of a lack of individual and governmental action toward policy and corporate pollution, or the inaction towards both, do not face any charges leaving marginalized families to figure out how to carry it alone.

Injustice will not only require temporary relief. We need meaningful change that requires real policies that address climate resilience alongside economic inequality. We need lasting investments in affordable housing, durable infrastructure, and equitable access to resources so that future disasters don't repeat the same story. Climate policies must be rooted in environmental justice and center the voices of frontline communities in planning and recovery efforts. Reparative actions such as direct cash aid, guaranteed housing, and debt relief must be prioritized to break the cycle of vulnerability. Until these changes are made, the same communities will continue to pay the price for a crisis they did not cause.

Academic Essays

The Effects Extreme Weather Has on Inequality Within the People

Adam Bastian, West Orange-Stark High School

The equality of a people is often drastically affected by times of extreme weather, but this most seen in impoverished communities as well as communities of marginalized groups such as African Americans and the lower middle class.

For instance, in 2021 when a massive ice storm occurred in southeast Texas it left most of the southeast of Texas without power and heating. Senator Ted Cruz left for Cancun while the rest of the people were here freezing and starving to death, but this is only one example. It's important to note that this tone of mistrust between the people and the government by saying that when the people are suffering the government cannot be counted on as a reliable entity to do its job of protecting the people.

As well we've seen that after various hurricanes, marginalized communities have been the last to receive aid from government organizations such as FEMA, instead favoring the wealthy upper middle-upper classes who already had resources available to them such as generators and running water. This shows us that in times of crisis the wealthy are the first to receive aid whereas those who are not wealthy and especially those who are not white are left to suffer while the rich white man is catered to first by the state.

In addition the very nature of extreme weather within a capitalist society such as the United States breeds inequality, and this has been true for hundreds of years such as in 1910 when a massive storm flooded the Mississippi River, so in order to stop the flooding the state used the bodies of African Americans as sand bags, as well refugees camps were set up for those who were displaced from the storm, however the whites were given first pick of housing and supplies, as well the black population within the camp were forced to perform hard labor, and when a black man tried to leave the police officers in the camp beat him. This proves again that only the wealthy whites are truly cared about by the state, further sowing distrust in the government's ability to serve its people.

Another instance of this inequality was during hurricane Ike when the city of New Orleans was destroyed, the first places that were given aid were the wealthy white neighborhoods, all while the poor black and Hispanic neighborhoods were left to wait in flood waters. This once again proves that in times of

81

extreme weather the wealthy are favored while the poor are left to suffer from the weather.

So in conclusion we see that time and time again the wealthy and the white are preferred to the poor and those who are non-white are left to suffer proving that in times of extreme weather crisis those of us who are poor and those of who are not white cannot count on our government to keep us safe when we need it most.

Barely Floating: Severe Weather and Inequality in Southeast Texas

Makaylee Dugan, Bridge City High School

People use the phrase "In the eye of a hurricane" to describe temporary peace, a break in the storm. For the families living in the Golden Triangle, when we reach the eye, we do not get peace; we simply must prepare for the warfare mother nature chooses to launch on us. Southeast Texas is no stranger to natural disasters, especially hurricanes and flash floods. These storms are a constant reminder of how vulnerable we are to nature's fury, and they are a reality we face every year. The region's struggles are compounded by the financial burden these disasters impose on families, which often go unaddressed by the systems that are supposed to help. According to FirstStreet.org, "The city of Bridge City has extreme risk from flooding. There are 4,153 properties in Bridge City at risk of flooding over the next 30 years. This represents 99.7% of all properties in Bridge City." This statistic is not just a number, it's the reality that thousands of families in this area live with every day. Hurricane season here is a dangerous time, and after each disaster, families are left scrambling to recover, sometimes for months or even years at a time.

Hurricane Ike, which hit in 2008, was the first major storm I can remember, even though I was only a few months old. I don't remember the hurricane itself, but I have vivid memories of my grandparents preparing for the storm. I can still picture them setting out sandbags, carrying in boxes of canned food, and making sure little me stayed far away from doors and windows. I also remember my grandmother's anxiety as she spoke to my mom about the destruction we were hearing about from neighbors who evacuated or had their homes destroyed. The Record describes the devastation: "Jerry Jones, city manager for Bridge City since 2000, says only 16 homes were untouched by what was measured as a 13-foot storm surge. That's out of about 3,000 homes. Texas Avenue was all water, like a big lake," he recalls. After the winds died down, recovery was difficult. "Even then, a heavy dump truck was required to make it over the Cow Bayou bridge from Orange... the water was halfway up the truck when we got to the bridge." That picture, of our town submerged in water, is burned into my memory, even though I was just a baby.

For my family, Hurricane Ike meant complete reconstruction. I'm fortunate that my grandfather, a contractor, was able to rebuild our home. His work has stood the test of time, but for many others, there was no one to help them put their lives back together. The damage was massive. Entire walls were torn out, and our chimney was destroyed. We were lucky that we had the resources to rebuild, but for many families in the area, recovery was not as easy. I've seen firsthand how hard it is for some families to bounce back after a storm, especially when resources are limited.

Then came Hurricane Laura in 2020. By this time, I was older, and I had a much clearer picture of what it meant to live through a hurricane. This storm was another reminder of the vulnerability of our area. My family evacuated to North Texas, and my dad stayed behind in Bridge City to watch over our house. While we were away, we were dealing with the stress of power outages and spoiled food. It took over a week to get the power back on. I remember coming back to school and noting the less energized, but instead exhausted and worn down appearances of my peers and instructors. Teachers were scrambling to catch up on lessons, and that wasn't the worst part. Laura came in the midst of the COVID-19 pandemic, which made the situation even worse. There was no quick return to normalcy. Many of my friends and neighbors were still struggling to recover, and I know people who are still dealing with the fallout from the storm. One of my aunts, for example, is still fighting with insurance companies to finish the repairs on her home—years later. This kind of prolonged recovery is something many in the area know all too well.

The financial strain that these disasters put on families is immense. Businesses are also hit hard, often unable to return to productivity, which adds to the economic stress. The interruption of daily life creates a ripple effect that extends far beyond just the immediate cleanup. My aunt's battle with insurance companies is just one example of how these systems fail families when they need help the most. The financial help that is supposed to be available after a disaster is often delayed, underfunded, or just plain inadequate, leaving many families to fend for themselves. The damage from these hurricanes and floods extends far beyond the physical destruction of property. The long-term financial burden on families is a key aspect of the inequality that exists in this region. Southeast Texas, and particularly Bridge City, is a place where extreme weather events are a constant threat, but the resources to handle these events are not equally available to everyone. The inequality here is clear: the families who are already struggling financially are the ones who bear the brunt of the disaster and the recovery process.

For many in the region, insurance is either insufficient or difficult to navigate. The process of rebuilding is often slowed down by insurance disputes, lack of coverage, and complicated bureaucratic hurdles. Families are left stuck in a cycle of waiting, rebuilding, and waiting again, while the cost of living continues to rise. The cycle of recovery becomes one of endless struggle, especially for those without the financial resources to bounce back. The stress of having to rebuild without enough support—both from the government and private insurers—only deepens the inequality felt by families in this area.

This constant uncertainty, the looming threat of another disaster, and the challenges of rebuilding after each one have a lasting impact. They create a sense of instability that makes it hard for anyone to feel truly secure. For the people of Southeast Texas, the threat of extreme weather is more than just an inconvenience, it is an ongoing reality that dictates the rhythm of daily life. And yet, despite the regularity of these storms, the systems in place to support recovery remain inadequate, leaving families to pick up the pieces on their own. Until the inequalities that plague this region arc addressed, the people of Southeast Texas will continue to live in the aftermath of disasters, fighting not just nature, but the systems that fail to protect them

The Storm Within: A Tale of Inequality and Extreme Weather

Brandi Evans, West Orange-Stark High School

Extreme weather events, such as hurricanes, floods, and droughts, have become increasingly common due to climate changes. These events do not only affect the environment but also increase the existing inequalities within society. This narrative explores the intersection of extreme weather and social disparity through the story of a community facing the aftermath of a devastating hurricane. However, in the small coastal town of Clearwater, life was simple yet vibrant. The community thrived on fishing and tourism, with families passing down their trades through generations. Although wealth was concentrated in the hands of a few, while many residents lived paycheck to paycheck, struggling to make ends meet, the local government, influenced by affluent business owners, often overlooked the needs of the less fortunate. As summer approaches, the whispers of an impending hurricane begin to circulate. The weather reports warned of a storm that could potentially be catastrophic. For example, while the wealthy prepared their homes with reinforced structures and stocked supplies, the poorer residents of Clearwater had no such luxury, they could only hope for the best, knowing that their homes were vulnerable and their resources limited. When Hurricane Maria struck, it was as if nature unleashed its wrath upon Clearwater. The winds howled, and the rain poured down in torrents, flooding the streets and uprooting trees. The storm left destruction in its wake, with homes damaged and lives shattered. In the aftermath, the stark contrast between the affluent and the impoverished became painfully evident. The wealthy residents, with their fortified homes, emerged relatively unscathed. They had the means to hire contractors and repair their properties swiftly. In contrast, the poorer families found themselves displaced, their homes rendered uninhabitable. Many sought refuge in shelters, where overcrowding and limited resources created a tense atmosphere. The inequality that had always existed was now laid bare for all to see. As the days turned into weeks, the recovery process began. The local government, overwhelmed by the scale of the disaster, struggled to provide adequate support. Aid arrived, but it was often misallocated, favoring those who had connections or wealth. The marginalized communities faced bureaucratic hurdles, making making it difficult for them to access the help desperately needed. In the heart of Clearwater, a grassroots movement emerged. Residents banded together, organizing food drives and distributing supplies to those in need. They recognized that their strength lay in unity, and they fought against the inequalities that had been exacerbated by the storm. Their resilience became a beacon of hope, illustrating the power of community in the face of adversity. Months later, as the town began to rebuild, the scars of the hurricane remained. However, the experience had sparked a change in perspective. The community realized that addressing inequality was not just a matter of charity but a necessity for a sustainable future. They advocated for policies that would ensure equitable access to resources, regardless of socioeconomic status. Although, the local government, pressured by the voices of its constituents, began to make changes. They prioritized infrastructure improvements in low-income neighborhoods and established programs to support small businesses. The community learned that resilience was not just about weathering the storm but also about creating a more just and equitable society. The story of Clearwater serves as a reminder of the profound impact of extreme weather on inequality. As climate change continues to threaten communities worldwide, it is crucial to recognize the interconnectedness of these issues. By addressing the root causes of inequality, we can build a more resilient future for all, ensuring that no one is left behind in the face of nature.

Untitled
Samantha Foreman, Little Cypress-Mauriceville High School

Natural disasters run rampant through our country daily. People's homes get flooded and destroyed, their roofs get taken away from strong winds, the ground's shake and shatter their personal belongings. It doesn't just take away their house, but a home built from the ground up with love. People must sit and watch as their house wastes away on the sidelines. However, these people are lucky.

It's sad to say that those whose homes have been taken due to a tragedy are lucky, but they are. For some, there is no house to be taken away. For some, there is no safe place, nothing to hold onto, and if they do have items, nowhere to store it. Each time there was a hurricane in Texas, I'd watch the schools asks around. They'd desperately ask the students if they needed help, money, food, anything just to keep them safe. They were lucky. These students were allowed to have hope, unlike our growing homeless population. The very people that us 'lucky' scoff and turn our nose at must fight for their life, and there is no relief or recognition for them. There is nowhere to run, no home to hide in, and nothing stopping the debris from smashing into you. Everyone has escaped, and now they are left behind to die. They cannot call for help. They just have to be lucky.

Luck isn't always there for all of us though. Sometimes everything you have is stripped away and you don't have the resources to get it back, and suddenly you are on the sidewalk too. Something as simple, yet horrifying, as not having enough money to rebuild your whole life at a moment's notice can, and will, bring you down and show you a new low. Even worse, people who have become homeless due to natural disaster statistically have it worse. August 29th , 2005, hurricane Katrina ripped through our nation ferociously. 200 thousand homes were lost to the disaster, 41 thousand being rented, which prices doubled after they were rebuilt. Many of the homeowners had paid off their mortgage but had not bothered to buy homeowner's insurance. Due to this, we had the largest displacement of people since the Dust Bowl, with about 800 thousand individuals having to move outside their home. Statistically, it gets even more horrifying. 60% of the New Orleans homeless population had lost their homes in Katrina, and the rate of homelessness is still growing in that area. Around 230 thousand jobs were lost, making it difficult to get the money they desperately needed back, and the severe mental health rate had gone up from 11% up to 14% directly after Katrina. So many factors, yet still, there's more.

If you were an interviewer, realistically you would want your best dressed, most confident, well groomed, and qualified for the job. You'd expect a good education stemming from high school up, along with an extensive resume showing where they've worked along with their skills and achievements, right? When all your clothes get taken away from a forest fire that spreads, and you can longer shower because you no longer have walls that'll stay upright, you won't be able to look your best. Not to mention, your job also got ripped away so you won't be able to get the money to buy new clothes or even get a gym membership just so you can shower. You have to look for a job, but you can't. You aren't dressed well enough for them. You don't even have an address to be billed to so for now, it's hopeless. However, your change cup is only collecting little bits every day, definitely not enough for a house, and barely enough to get your calories in for the day. Would've been lucky to get some of that disaster relief money, right?

..Right?

Your disaster relief is being defunded. Hundreds of staff at the Federal Emergency Management Agency (FEMA) have been terminated, and continue to be terminated. FEMA works to make sure that people are prepared for disasters, support long-term recovery, people get their insurance money, and hazards are reduced. They're targeting national preparedness, grants, hazard mitigation, and flood insurance and mitigation directorates. This will heavily affect our country, but especially Texas. In the end, the defunding feels like a cruel joke. It's been only a few months since the devastating floods in Kentucky and West Virginia. The people who need help the most right now are dying, and we are only worsening it.

Extreme Weather and Inequality
Morgan Haynes, Little Cypress-Mauriceville High School

Extreme weather events, including hurricanes, floods, wildfires, and heatwaves, have increased in frequency and intensity due to climate change. These events often exacerbate existing inequalities, disproportionately impacting low-income communities, marginalized populations, and those without the resources to recover. Enhancing preparedness for extreme weather can significantly reduce its devastating effects on these vulnerable groups.

Extreme weather has an extensive history, but its impacts are increasingly visible in modern society. Natural disasters have traditionally been viewed as equalizers that affect everyone alike. However, recent events have revealed stark differences in how different communities are affected and how quickly they can recover. For instance, Hurricane Katrina in 2005 tragically illustrated how inequalities can shape disaster outcomes. New Orleans's poorer neighborhoods suffered the brunt of the storm, revealing issues related to infrastructure and response systems that affected marginalized groups. This pattern of inequality in disaster impact is not limited to a single event but replicates across the globe, highlighting just how affected they are.

The current context of extreme weather is influenced by climate change, which is primarily driven by human activities. According to the Intergovernmental Panel on Climate Change, more frequent and severe weather events are projected for the coming decades. For example, the increasing intensity of wildfires in California has resulted in greater property damage and deaths with the poorest communities often finding themselves trapped in harm's way due to inadequate resources. The health implications of extreme heat in urban areas also show how the elderly, low-income groups, and racial minorities can suffer disproportionately.

Many individuals and organizations have taken significant strides in addressing these challenges. Activists such as Greta Thunberg and organizations like the Sunrise Movement have brought climate justice to the forefront of public discussion. Their advocacy stresses the need to center the voices of marginalized communities in climate discussions. Policy makers such as the New York Governor, Andrew Cuomo, have also recognized the importance of addressing inequality in disaster readiness. After Hurricane Sandy in 2012, there was a united effort to include social justice in the planning and implementation of recovery measures.

These developments signal a growing awareness that disaster preparedness must consider social disparities.

Different perspectives exist regarding the best approaches to improving preparedness for extreme weather events. Some advocate for top-down policy reforms, emphasizing infrastructure improvements, emergency management changes, and enhanced public investment in vulnerable communities. For instance, redesigning buildings to withstand floods or creating green spaces to reduce urban heat can safeguard communities against specific weather events. Others argue for grassroots approaches, highlighting the importance of community-based resilience. Initiatives such as neighborhood preparedness workshops and local emergency response teams can empower communities to respond effectively to disasters.

An essential component of preparedness is education. Teaching individuals about climate change, its associated risks, and available recovery resources builds community resilience. For example, schools can incorporate climate education into their curriculum to raise awareness among younger generations. Furthermore, engaging communities in simulations and drills can improve readiness for future weather events. These activities allow residents to understand emergency protocols and foster a spirit of collaboration in crisis response.

Improving communication systems also plays a critical role in disaster preparedness. Many low-income communities suffer from inadequate access to information during extreme weather events. Innovations in technology can bridge this gap. Developing free apps that provide real-time updates on weather conditions, emergency services, and shelter availability can empower individuals to make informed decisions. Additionally, targeted outreach in vulnerable communities ensures that everyone receives the necessary information, regardless of their socio-economic status.

Investment in sustainable infrastructure is crucial for long-term preparedness. Governments and organizations can prioritize equitable access to resources, such as reliable public transportation and adequate healthcare facilities, which can significantly aid recovery efforts. Programs that leverage public-private partnerships can also help ensure that resources are allocated efficiently to the communities that need them most. For example, renewable energy initiatives can lead to job creation while also fortifying local economies against the impacts of extreme weather.

Future developments and innovations are necessary to ensure that preparedness strategies evolve alongside changing climate conditions. Continuous research into the interactions between weather extremes and social inequalities will provide a more nuanced understanding of the issues at hand. Policymakers must remain adaptable, using data-driven approaches to tailor their responses to the specific challenges that arise as the climate crisis unfolds.

In conclusion, the link between extreme weather and inequality is a pressing issue requiring immediate attention. The awareness that extreme weather affects communities differently compels society to improve preparedness. By focusing on education, communication, grassroots initiatives, and sustainable infrastructure, society can work toward a more equitable future. As climate change continues to challenge the status quo, fostering resilience among the most vulnerable will be crucial in mitigating the impact of extreme weather events.

Works Cited

Intergovernmental Panel on Climate Change. "Climate Change 2021: The Physical Science Basis." Cambridge University Press, 2021.

Thunberg, Greta. "No One Is Too Small to Make a Difference." Penguin, 2019.

Seymour, D. "Preparing for Future Weather Events: A Community-Based Approach." Environmental Justice Journal, vol. 12, no. 3, 2020, pp. 115–123.

Impact of Climate Change in Impoverished Communities

Baylee Lowe, West Orange-Stark High School

As climate change continues to worsen year by year, so do natural disasters all around the world. Disasters such as hurricanes, tornadoes, flooding, and wildfires are all heavily impacted by the devastating rise of climate change, and the effects of these disasters are seen in their aftermaths, leaving people injured and killed, and with homes and communities destroyed. In these disastrous events, everyone is impacted in some form or another, but the most impacted communities consist of impoverished, marginalized, and underdeveloped areas. These communities in particular have been statistically proven to be more at risk and affected by natural disasters, for reasons ranging from income, infrastructure, and environmental racism. It's important, however, to analyze exactly how these communities themselves came to be, and why exactly they're at risk, to study the history of these areas and how they relate to the world today.

Looking at victims of natural disasters in America, high percentages of affected communities are made up of mostly Black and Hispanic Americans, as well as Indigenous communities. Jim Crow laws of the 1900's along with segregation and redlining played crucial roles in this statistic. After the Emancipation Proclamation was signed in 1865, many institutions and buildings, such as schools and homes for people of color, were required to be built. This did not mean they were in similar conditions to White populated buildings. When comparing the two, one can clearly see how Black institutions were built with flimsy, wooden planks compared to the durable bricks of White schoolhouses. This noticeable difference in infrastructure would last for decades well into the late 90's, and even the present day, resulting in the legacy of Black Americans living in more rundown and uncared-for areas as opposed to the pristine suburbs that White Americans populated. The exclusivity of suburbs were more openly available for White Americans, and almost impossible to obtain as a person of color. Redlining was a major cause of forming densely populated neighborhoods with minorities, as it was usually the only option.

These neighborhoods in question have low-quality infrastructure and are much easier to destroy in times of extreme weather conditions. Combined with the already existing systematic racism in America, it is no wonder that minority areas are one of the most at-risk populations in times of disaster. This all isn't just to say that

93

people of color are more likely to directly be affected by climate change, but also that the consequences and the aftermath of these events are much more dire. Studies regarding minority communities and the aftermath of natural disasters showed that Hispanic and Black Americans were much more likely to not be returned to their homes, or displaced. Lower incomes play a role in dealing with the effects of natural disasters, of which Hispanic, Black, and Indigenous populations make up the majority of the poverty census in America. Discrimination is also still alive and well, and these communities face it even during times like these. Disaster response organization, FEMA, has faced multiple reports of providing less governmental assistance to marginalized communities as opposed to their White counterparts, as well as having increased denial rates for low-income applicants.

Although minorities are specifically more susceptible to more damage in extreme weather conditions, much of it has to do with poverty and low income, which are unfortunate conditions that mostly people of color experience. Low-income communities face disparities such as food and water shortages due to crop failure and changes in precipitation, pollution from the air, outbreak of diseases, and disruptions within important factors of life such as careers which impact the ability to make income. I myself have witnessed and experienced these factors in my own community. My area is what would be described as a low-income community, and my school is right in the middle of a multitude of plants. You can smell the disgusting odors coming from the plants throughout the day, and the air quality index sits high almost every day. In the face of disasters, my community experiences it harder than areas like Beaumont or Houston. During the hurricane of 2020, Hurricane Laura was devastating for my town and the entirety of the Gulf Coast, resulting in billions of dollars in damages and at least the deaths of seventy people. I sustained damages to my own house when my family's ceiling collapsed in two places caused by debris and branches falling due to harsh winds. Getting the repairs for the house took a long period of time with construction beginning in September and only getting finished seven months later in April. Alongside dealing with repairs, impoverished areas also face the struggles of evacuation, confronted with an unexpected need for money to obtain gas, food, and temporary shelter.

Low-income communities are then stuck within the cycle of poverty with each natural disaster combatted. People are forced to find ways to support themselves financially during the aftermath of these situations, while also trying to use money to fix their areas. It can almost seem like no matter how much you save or work for, the effects of extreme weather only pull you back down into losing anything that you managed to save, leaving you with nothing all over again. So, how can we fix this, and is it even possible? Well, yes, but only if people are willing to stand up for these communities, and only if these communities are able to stand with each other as well. Of course, the power of unity isn't going to solve all these issues, and it's up to our government and city officials to address these issues and create ways to fix them. Implementing more affordable housing, durable infrastructure, financial opportunities, awareness of environmental racism, access to healthcare, and ensuring that aid programs and disaster recovery groups are equally distributed are all ways to begin creating a better future for these marginalized and disadvantaged areas.

Ultimately, it's clear to see how extreme weather affects everybody, but when looking at these examples and studying the disparities of minority groups compared to majority groups, it is evident that people of color and people in poverty are more likely to experience more difficult evacuation and recovery, and are more impacted. These disparities are worsened by low income, poor urban planning and environments, unsustainable infrastructure for harsh weather, unequal treatment from aid organizations, and lack of opportunities. The world has many steps to take to fix these issues and it will take these communities staying strong and communicating with political officials to get real change made. Above all this, the true root issue is climate change itself, and with each day further and further we reach the inability to go back from the massive amount of damage already done to our planet. Steps that can be taken to reduce your carbon footprint and damage to the Earth include conserving energy, moving away from fossil fuels, investing in renewable energy, and supporting the fight against climate change. It is important to stress the steps of taking action for our world, so events like these don't occur or if they do, these disasters are not so severe or life-threatening.

Hurricanes Hurt More When You're Black
Aaron Miller, West Orange-Stark High School

Before World War II, the 9th ward experienced very significant population changes, because of racial segregation and the impact of the industrial canal, a canal that was excavated in 1918 that provided a shortcut for ships that let them bypass the Mississippi river and allowed easy access to the Gulf of Mexico. The canal and bridges associated with it like the St. Claude Avenue Bridge led to a massive growth and development in the 9th ward, before the canal was finished the 9th ward was a sparsely populated area with farmlands and swamplands, this place was populated with poor white and black laborers. Formerly enslaved people settled in the 9th ward in areas like Fazendeville. While racial tensions were still a thing there was no strict segregation laws yet. In 1923 after the canal was fully finished, it attracted many people interested in working in the industries, this included a lot of white workers who were mostly Irish and German immigrants, due to this increase in white workers new subdivisions of houses were built for them like the Holy Cross Neighborhood in the Upper 9th ward near the canal.

By 1940 the 9th ward was 70% white. After World War II ended in 1945, Black people migrated to the 9th ward in search of cheap housing and wartime jobs, but due to the violent redlining they were confined to the lower 9th ward, even so the white flight still started in the 9th ward. In fear of racial integration and loans from the federal housing association that let them move into suburbs white people either moved out the 9th ward or concentrated on living in the subdivision neighborhoods built for them in the upper 9th ward. By 1960 the lower 9th ward was almost 65% Black. This number grew even higher in 1970s-2000s because of blockbusting, a practice in which realtors scare homeowners likely using racial stereotypes to scare them into selling their house for a cheaper price. By 2000 the lower 9th ward was over 95% black, although it was one of the poorest it was only of the most culturally vibrant areas in New Orleans.

In 2004, the lower 9th ward became a vibrant working-class black neighborhood due to the cheap housing. It was the centerpiece of black ownership and housing; the lower 9th was a densely populated area with many residents with the population count being near the 14,000 range. They celebrated many unique holidays like St. Joseph's night, where families built three tiered alters that held delicious foods like, bread shaped like fish, fava beans, and red wine. These alters also contained photos of dead family members; you were forced to take a fava bean when you left because it was considered to be bad luck to leave without one. This is just one of the many traditions the lower 9th ward had.

On August 23, 2005, Hurricane Katrina formed over the Bahamas as a "tropical depression" basically a cluster of unorganized thunderstorms. August 24, 2005, the "cluster of storms" turned into a category 1 hurricane and was formerly named hurricane Katrina. Two days later on August 26, 2005, the hurricane swelled into a category 3 storm basically overnight. While this took place the media constantly downplayed the actual damage Katrina could cause, like Brian Williams who was on NBC news nightly saying, "This storm could be 'the big one' for New Orleans, but let's not overreact flooding is likely to be 'manageable' in most areas". This was just one day after the hurricane swelled on August 27, 2005. While the media downplayed Katrina the residents of lower 9th ward had no faith in the levees built to hold off floods. The residents had seen near misses before like Hurricane Betsy, a powerful category 4 hurricane that struck in 1965, a knew that the levees were poorly maintained. The tension and unease that formed in the 9th ward led to a giant evacuation crisis. The city's evacuation plan relied on cars but the lower 25% of residents in the 9th ward had no vehicles, there was no public transit shutdown plan. This led to over 200buses being parked in low lying parking lots instead of being used to evacuate people. Officials made the superdome a "shelter", but it had no supplies and no backup electricity, the residents who were unlucky to stay there even brough lawn chairs and diapers knowing how terrible it'd be.

August 28, 2005, Hurrican Katrina grew to a category 5 many people prayed while others boarded their houses. August 29, 6:10am, Katrina makes landfall east of New Orleans as a category 3, it's weaker than expected but the water kept rising. 9am of August 29th A 30-foot wall of water bursts through the levee made to protect the lower 9th ward. This wave crushed the houses in minutes. It was so loud that residents who heard it described it as "a sound like a freight train". Families axed through their roofs to get to safety, they were stuck up there for days on end with no help in sight. Helicopters circled overhead but prioritized wealthier, whiter areas of New Orleans. The lower 9th ward has been underwater for 3 days at this point with no organized rescue prepared. After 5 days of being stuck on top of their houses, 5 days with no food or water, 5 days without basic utilities and human necessities, the first organized rescue arrived in the lower 9th ward. The "organized rescue" that arrived treated the little remaining survivors as criminals, calling them looters and thieves. There were police blockades that turned around black survivors with guns to pointed at them claiming that they were threats. Dead bodies floated in the water; it was hell on earth. The damage was so bad that buried slaves and native Americans from decades ago were surfaced and seen floating through the water. The media of course use this tragedy to dehumanize and put down the black residents of the lower 9th ward, with Fox News using a picture of Black people wading through water with the caption "Looters Run Wild." They were scavenging for food for their starving children. The FEMA director Micheal Brown went on record and said that "People are suffering because they chose not to evacuate." even though zero buses were sent to the 25% percent of residents who didn't own a vehicle. The media even went as far as covering up the death toll with them saying it was only 1,400 people who died but there were over 200 dead bodies in the 9th ward alone who went unnamed.

Hurricane Katrina was not just a hurricane, it was a weapon used to exterminate and kill the black residents of the 9th ward, with the widely known unmaintained levees all the way to the helicopters being told to focus on privileged parts of the 9th ward. This is just one of the many cases where Hurricanes hurt black people more, until systematic change happens these events will continue to happen and continue to rip innocent Black people from their families. As a person of color I've sadly been victim to this same thing that happened to the people in the 9th ward. When hurricane Harvey, a category 4 hurricane hit Orange Texas, I didn't own a car so the only choice I had was to bunker down throughout the storm. I was lucky enough to come out with my house and family still intact but because of the redlining that goes on in orange I know people who were under the same circumstances I was and not come out as lucky as I was.

The deaths caused by these hurricanes were unnecessary and could have been prevented if we had the change that allowed minorities to evacuate or earn enough money to be able to properly evacuate in times of need, but I feel that America is far from that dream I have, I'll still try my hardest to make sure it comes true.

Inequality
Athan R. Peterson, Vidor High School

Inequality can provide large impacts into the world. But these impacts affect everyone in a very negative way. With natural disasters, they cause deaths. Human lives; just thrown away, because the damage was too reckless and they weren't economically stable enough to stay safe. Even some of the people who keep their lives are still affected negatively since their houses may just get wiped off the face of the Earth, causing homelessness. Through homelessness, inequality can come about. Bad apples within the higher classes of society see homeless people as "lower beings" and treat them more differently than they would toward someone that they see as equal. This can cause worse effects to come about through things like the general population, who is easily influenced by higher figures, to jump on a bandwagon of mistreatment towards the less fortunate. This can build mass amounts of resentment towards the riches, not just the bad riches, but all riches, since people can build stereotypes towards whole groups of people instead of just the bad apples. This happens so much in the real world. Ironically enough; the "bad" rich people mistreat the poor simply because of their own stereotypes towards the less fortunate since they make up a relatively large portion of crime. From "R Street Institute", they found that homeless individuals make up 6-8% of all crimes, and worse, 11-15% of violent crimes. It can be a cycle of constant resentment between classes, which can cause a consistent increase in inequality between the individuals.

Separately, on the plate of inequality, it has grown to be an issue for everyone. Racism, sexism, ageism: these are the major unequal spaces within the everyday world. Through racism, people have stereotypes of African Americans, Arabic, indigenous, etc. Stereotypes of violence and crime, just because, again, "bad apples" caused deadly events to occur. After analysis, you start to notice a pattern. Inequality is caused by profiled stereotypes of the minority. Furthermore, you'll be able to assess this:

- Sexism: Men think women are unable to do the jobs that men can do, and even if they accomplish it, they get paid less.
- Sexuality sexism: Outcasted because of who they love or how they identify.
- Ageism: People assume that older and younger people do not have the experience or capability to complete the jobs of anyone who is experienced and capable at their prime.

Inequalities within the world can cause so much pain and suffering through unfair treatment and absolute disrespect. We as people need to realize that not everyone is bad, and that everyone deserves a chance, until they prove they have destroyed that chance. No one, and I mean NO ONE, should be casted away or disrespected based off of just a first glance. Too much death, and violence, and suicide has been committed as a result of this ignorance that judges a book based on the cover. We must find the common ground to become better people. People who can realize the most important fact of all: We are all human.

Weather & Inequality

Natalie Smith, Bridge City High School

Historically, people of color have been treated unequally. This inequality is highlighted in severe weather events. Research shows that people of color are affected more severely by flooding and climate change than those of the majority, with mental and physical health being key factors to examine. Those of color are more susceptible to trauma due to flooding being more common in colored communities, as well as hereditary diseases unable to be treated. It is important to review and acknowledge these struggles so that they may be reflected on and addressed correctly.

Mental health plays a huge part in these cases of minority vs majority. Studies have shown that colored communities tend to flood more severely than white communities. The International Journal of Disaster Risk Reduction stated that "...minoritized populations often experience the most severe disaster exposures, as they are more likely to live in flood-prone areas and have fewer residents with access to a reliable vehicle with which to evacuate...." This is a stressor not common amongst white communities, which in turn causes a rise in cases of trauma and/or depression in these minority communities. These communities are separated most frequently due to color or income. If these communities were not separated, the issue could be fixed. Therefore, the solution to lower these cases in minorities would be to end the separation between minority and majority communities. Another solution would be to better fund these minority communities so that when flooding does happen, their houses are well protected, and they have secure methods of evacuation. Lastly, as a country, the government could take the effort and time to prevent houses from flooding in minority communities by elevating houses or building on elevated land. Minorities are commonly put in danger or become sick during extreme weather, leading to issues in physical health and minorities attempting to afford healthcare.

Physical health is a harder situation to correct, but it can be done. The National Library of Medicine states, "For racial and ethnic minorities in the United States, health disparities take on many forms, including higher rates of chronic disease and premature death compared to the rates among whites." While it is important to note that this is not universal, it is still an issue that must be addressed. Naturally occurring events due to climate change, such as heat waves, also affect people of color more severely than white people. Two separate issues are retaining the health of minorities.

Those issues include the previously stated climate change and access to healthcare. A study conducted by Harvard University concludes that while chronic diseases are more common in people of a minority than the majority, the real issue is the inequality these minorities face. A quote from Williams and Lavizzio-Moruey states, "Where we live determines opportunities to access high-quality education, employment, housing, fresh foods or outdoor space–all contributors to our health." All of which have been observed to be drastically different for minorities as they struggle to obtain proper funds for basic healthcare, let alone extensive treatment for chronic diseases. These issues can be solved by making healthcare more obtainable to minorities. This can be done by making government pay, such as social security, more sustainable. On the other end of the spectrum, the government could partially fund healthcare with tax money to make it more affordable for those struggling with funds. Another issue in this category would be the reason minorities struggle to obtain funds. Jobs, while prohibited from discrimination, are catered more towards citizens of the majority population. Those who do not speak English are forced to learn an entirely new dialect just to put food on the table. The U.S should develop more jobs for minorities who struggle with, don't speak, or are still learning English to work. This would allow these minorities to afford necessities such as basic and extensive healthcare.

In conclusion, discrimination is the big issue we face today relating to weather-based health in minorities. Addressing these issues is the only proper way to discover a fix for them. Without acknowledging the discrimination these minorities still face in the modern day, the inequalities will persist. Therefore, the first step to change is acknowledgement. If we can acknowledge and solve these issues, we may very well create a better and more equity-based world for everyone.

About the Project's Sponsors:

Ancient to the Future

The Ancient to the Future Project is a small think tank working to tackle inequality and climate crisis by combining and amplifying local voices. This means discussions, publications, and creativity. "Ancient to the Future" is a prophetic idea from the Art Ensemble of Chicago. In full: "We Must Be Ancient to the Future to Survive."

- Kate Williams, Executive Director

The Center for History and Culture of Southeast Texas and the Upper Gulf Coast

Founded in 2016 by Dr. Mary Scheer, the Center for History and Culture serves Lamar University students and faculty, the communities of Southeast Texas and the greater Gulf, and the scholars and creatives who explore the region's past, present, and future. The Center promotes the study and creativity of these regions with a commitment to multicultural, interdisciplinary, collaborative, and community-focused projects.

- Jimmy Bryan, Director

Acknowledgements

This anthology would not have been possible without the generosity, enthusiasm, and collaboration of the many educators and administrators who supported this project across Orange County. We extend our deepest gratitude to Dr. Amanda James of Bridge City High School, Principal Dart of Vidor High School, Principal Wrinkle of Orangefield High School, Principal Amber Hawk of Little Cypress-Mauriceville High School, and Principal Holifield of West Orange-Stark High School for their encouragement and support in making this project accessible to their students.

We are especially grateful to the English teachers and department chairs who helped bring this opportunity into their classrooms. At Bridge City High School, special thanks go to Mrs. Sylvia Ney for her help in sharing materials and guiding student writers. At Vidor High School, Mrs. Sanderson's enthusiasm and classroom participation were instrumental in generating student interest. At Orangefield High School, Mr. Ronald Chevalier provided essential coordination with the English Department and student body. At Little Cypress-Mauriceville, the English Department as a whole offered valuable collaboration and encouragement to their students. At West Orange-Stark High School, Ms. Monica Guillory's communication and support helped ensure student participation.

For the development and publication of this anthology, I would like to extend special thanks to Ellen Walker Rienstra, Ron Rozelle, and County Judge Gothia for their time and effort in reviewing these works.

We also thank the Center for History and Culture at Lamar University for funding the publication of this anthology and providing Lamar University Literary Press the opportunity to recognize these talented young writers during their Fall Launch event.

And to those who were perhaps most instrumental in bringing this anthology to life—a heartfelt thank you to Katherine Hoerth, Theresa Ener, and Kate Williams. Their guidance, patience, and creative insight made possible the printed work you now hold in your hands.

And to my dad, Donald Harmon: thank you for your endless support, local know-how, and for somehow knowing *everyone* in Orange County. I could not have done this without you.

Finally, to the students of Orange County—thank you for your creativity, courage, and honesty. Your words remind us of the power of storytelling and connecting with our communities.